How to make NEWSLETTERS, BROCHURES, & OTHER GOOD STUFF without a computer system

Handbook on promotion planning, writing, and pasteup for small business and more

by H. Gregory

PINSTRIPE PUBLISHING

HOW TO MAKE NEWSLETTERS, BROCHURES, &
OTHER GOOD STUFF WITHOUT A COMPUTER SYSTEM

Handbook on promotion planning, writing,
and pasteup for small business and more.

by H. Gregory

FIRST PRINTING, 1987

Published by
    PINSTRIPE PUBLISHING
    Post Office Box 157
    Kenmore, WA   98028

ISBN 0-941973-01-8
Library of Congress Catalog Card Number 87-61139

HF
5825
G675
1987

MANUFACTURED IN THE UNITED STATES OF AMERICA

Contents

Introduction

Do you need to create some promotional material? A newsletter? A price list?

"Advertising can be valuable," according to the Small Business Administration in its Small Business Bibliography <u>Marketing for Small Business</u>, "but in many cases advertisements in newspapers, television, etc., are too expensive for small businesses. Direct mail to key customers is frequently suggested."

In these pages you will share in first-hand experience learning layout, photos, artwork, the content and writing of copy, printing, and mailing. A checklist at the end of each chapter provides an easy way to "brush up" between mailings, and illustrations throughout the book are used not only to organize basic information and help you become familiar with it, but also to make it easier for you to find that information when you need it.

You'll learn some basic why's and when's of promotion, as well as tips on graphic aids, how to use them, and where to find them. Learn to reproduce photographs on a copy machine with good results, Learn where to find artwork or how to make your own. Learn

how to write a press release. Learn when the
best times for mailing are, and how to tell
when you're ready for bulk mail rates.

If you can learn to "think on paper" and
follow a few rules, you can increase your
chances of success. One rule is to have
a good product or service. Another is
what specific information must absolutely
be in any advertising or promotional mailer
you do. Yet another rule is to have consistency in your mailings.

Statistics show that direct mail works—
look at all the pieces in your mail box!
Your mailer can become lost in that volume
unless it is different. It must be something
that your customer will recognize and read.
It must reflect your personality and your
product in a way that will motivate the
reader to respond. It doesn't have to be
"slick" to do the job, and may work better
because it's not.

From the blank page to the finished
camera-ready mechanical, "HOW TO MAKE NEWS-
LETTERS, BROCHURES, AND OTHER GOOD STUFF"
will show you how to write copy and create
layouts—no computer needed!

Acknowledgements

My thanks to the following for their kind assistance and interest in the making of this handbook.

Contributions consisted of information, artwork, and illustrations, with information to be sent to readers of this book upon request.

Avery International
Dick Blick
Creative Media Services
Dot Pasteup Supply
Dynamic Graphics
Graphic Products Corporation
Letraset USA
P O Instrument Company
The Printers Shopper
Konica Business Machines USA
Polycor Corporation
U. S. Postal Service
Zipatone

In addition, my thanks and appreciation goes to Mike and Mary for their support and encouragement.

Helen Gregory

ABOUT THE AUTHOR...

   Helen Gregory is a Seattle writer with over
twenty years experience in the business world, having
served as Office Manager-Controller of a retail corporation for ten years before heading up her own
retail store.

   While managing that store, Ms. Gregory dis-
covered the value of newsletters and flyers to area
merchants, and began to research the impact of
private mailings. She found that most merchants
got better results with informal direct mailings
than from expensive media advertising.

   This book, then, is NOT the recorded theories
of a classroom-bound professor, but rather the
hands-on experience of one who fought in the
trenches of a retailing war; one who paid for
uniforms and weapons with borrowed capital and
the proverbial pound of flesh; one who marched;
then fell; then rose again to reach a
calculated Peace.

   Ms. Gregory offers here some "tricks of the
trade" to use in producing your own promotional
materials, how often to send them, what they MUST
contain, how to design them, and the most economical way to get them printed and mailed.

WARNING! DISCLAIMER!

This book is not designed to be an absolute comprehensive guide to promotion or graphic arts, but to give the beginner a place to start in producing his own promotional materials.

Although extensive research was done in compiling the information, the author and publisher assume no responsibility for errors, inaccuracies, omissions, or any other inconsistency herein. It is by no means a substitute for professional or legal advice, and no guarantee of success is implied or given. Any slights against persons or organizations are unintentional.

1 Getting Started

I once searched the newspaper for fire-wood ads and found an appealing one. It had a nice line drawing, very fair price, and the right type and size of wood. I wanted to respond, but there was NO ADDRESS OR PHONE NUMBER!

Seems simple and understated, but it happens! Every mailout you send, every advertisement you place, MUST have your name (business), location (address), phone number, and business hours. It must also give a benefit to the customer.

How do you do that? Start with a blank piece of paper. Just as professional writers make many rewrites or drafts, your blank page will NOT be a final, camera-ready copy. What it WILL be is your "thinking on paper." A worksheet.

As you follow the recommendations outlined in this book, you will reach your final draft automatically, then transform it into a black and white camera-ready page for the photocopy machine or printer. That black and white camera-ready page is called a "mechanical," and here's how you start it—by "thinking on paper."

1. FIND A BLANK PIECE OF PAPER. It can be expensive 100% rag stationery with gold trim, a paper napkin, or maybe the back of a paper placemat at the Chinese Restaurant. I often use the latter! Call this paper your "worksheet."

2. FIND A PEN OR PENCIL. Something that will write on your paper. I always carry a small spiral notebook with a pen clipped into the spiral. Ideas are fleeting, and MUST BE noted at the time they pass through your conciousness. Now comes the time to start writing on that blank paper! But what?

3. ASK YOURSELF THIS QUESTION: "What is my current need, or problem?" Your current need may also be your long term need—that is, do you need to do something about it right away (current) or do you need to do something over a period of months (long term)?

You may have more than one need, so jot down all that come to mind. Usually your biggest need or problem is the one which comes to mind first, and for which you must begin a solution. Perhaps you need money. Perhaps you need time. Or a pat on the back. WRITE IT DOWN!

No matter how improperly worded, misspelled, or silly it seems, WRITE IT DOWN! You must define your needs, or problems if you are to find any ideas for solving them. Needs can be stated in just a few words, and writing them down leaves your brain free to work on a solution. Don't waste your valuable time trying to recall your basic need, which is also your purpose for making a promotional mailer.

WRITING IT DOWN is a crucial step in building that mailer.

4. STUDY YOUR NEEDS. Now that you can see them on paper, study your needs. Can any be combined? Do you see the same under-lying reason for all or many of them—such as "running out of money?" Perhaps your problem is the church picnic, and you must prepare 100 flyers to be posted, inviting the public to join your group. "What's so hard about that?" you ask. "Just scrawl a few words on paper, have it copied, and hang it up!"

Sure. It might work. But with a little "thinking on paper" and <u>purposeful placement</u> of that information, the $6.00 or so you spend for copying can bring twice the results or better.

Study your needs. Think about them, not only from your viewpoint, but also from your customer's. As you change back and forth from your perspective to your customer's, ideas will spring up in your mind for solving them.

5. NOTE YOUR ALTERNATIVE SOLUTIONS. All problems or needs have more than one solution. Maybe not all are plausible, maybe some even ridiculous (it helps), but write them all down. Just as you wrote down your needs, no matter how silly sounding or incorrectly spelled, now list your alternative for solving them.

For example, if you are a small retailer who is running short of operating capital, you might answer your need (running out of money) with these alternatives:

(a) rob a bank
(b) try for a loan
(c) ask friends or relatives
(d) have a dilly of a sale

6. CHOOSE A SOLUTION. The easiest way to choose a solution is by the process of elimination. Right away you can start crossing off your alternatives, beginning with "rob a bank," because you really had no intention of robbing a bank! Nor do you have the time.

A better solution might be to try for a loan at the bank. But, if your need for money is IMMEDIATE, answer (b) will not be the solution unless you are already set up on the quick-loan ticket. Or get the loan and forget the mailer.

Your pride keeps you from letting friends and relatives know what a financial bind you are in, so forget (c). Maybe you choose NOT to go further into debt at this time.

You are left with (d) "have a dilly of a sale." Somewhere in your bones you knew all along that to have a sale was the only correct answer. Get rid of merchandise that will soon be outdated or shopworn. But now comes another question: "What kind of sale to have?" and "How to let people know about it?" You send out an announcement. A mailer.

If you've decided this is a one-time mailer, skim through Chapter Two right now and read the paragraphs on "flyers." After reading that, go right on to the chapter on Layout and Design.

When your flyer is in the mail and you consider a long-term promotion schedule, read the chapter on Planning Promotions.

There is much good reading offered by the Small Business Administration regarding management and promotion of small business. Write to them at P. O. Box 15434, Ft. Worth, Texas 76119, and request these two pamphlets and order forms:

No. 115A "Business Development Pamphlets"

No. 115B "Business Development Booklets"

When your order forms arrive, be sure to order, from 115A, a pamphlet titled "Home Business." It is an in-depth listing of books, newsletters, and associations covering a wide range of small businesses.

S U M M A R Y

1. Define your problem/need and study it.

2. List alternative solutions.

3. Eliminate solutions that won't work.

4. Pencil-in your name, address, phone, and business hours on your worksheet.

5. Send for SBA pamphlets.

2 Formats & Other Good Stuff

Format is the style, image, or "look" that your mailer has. Before you decide what format to use, read through the following descriptions of different types of mailers. Some require more "copy" (text, writing) than others, and that may have a bearing on your decision.

Keep in mind that more pages mean more cost. Your purpose is to notify customers economically but effectively. Your mailer wants to be uniquely you, easy to recognize. It must identify your product or service, yet be something you can afford to maintain. You will want to produce it on a regular basis.

Develop a "look" and stay with it; consistency is the key to promotion.

C O U P O N S

Coupons may be printed several to a page, or separately and included in a larger mailer. If you use a single coupon printed directly on your mailer, place it on an outside corner, never in the center where readers hesitate to cut it out.

A coupon MUST show a benefit to the customer. Giving away a free item or a specific amount of money off outpulls coupons that require an additional purchase. For best results, feature a frequently used item (disposable, like toilet tissue, or consumable, like bread). Coupons are good to use when opening a new store or service. State the qualifications and restrictions boldly. Always state the expiration date—sooner for low budget items and longer, like 30 days, for high priced items. Customers may have to save up enough money for a high priced item, so they'll need more time to take advantage of your offer.

The purpose of a coupon is to get customers into your store to try your product or service. Direct mail coupons reap about seven percent more return than coupons placed in newspapers.

Be sure all of your regular customers know of your coupon—otherwise they may feel slighted and never return! Also make sure that all your sales help know about the coupon—what the offer is, any conditions, and expiration. Nothing is so depressing as to bring new customers into your store and let an unknowing sales clerk spoil the opportunity at hand.

F L Y E R S

A flyer, sometimes spelled flier, is a single page, printed on one or both sides with your promotional material. It can include a coupon, and usually carries artwork, large informal print (you may hand letter a flyer) and very often is printed on colored paper. Flyers can be stuffed into envelopes or simply folded, addressed on a blank side, and mailed.

A flyer can be used for a hand-out to people passing by, or put on car windshields (get permission from the parking lot owners), posted on bulletin boards, or taped in a window (again, get permission if it is not your window!).

WINDOW SIGNS & POSTERS

Kits can be purchased to make window signs and posters. One such supplier is New England Business Service (NEBS). Or you can make them by hand on large paper or illustration board.

Use bright colors—red is good to draw the eye, especially on yellow paper or illustration board (available at artists' supply or craft supply shops). Keep window signs and posters easy to read and uncluttered.

P A M P H L E T S

A pamphlet is a short, two page piece most often on a single topic. There is no binding or staples used, but rather it is printed on an 8½"x11" paper folded into thirds, or on 11"x17" paper folded in half to 8½"x11" and then folded again into thirds for mailing.

Pamphlets are very often done in full color, promoting a product line.

B R O C H U R E S

From a single folded page to a stapled or foldout multipage piece, brochures often carry full color photos on slick paper.

Sending a "slick" color brochure infers that you are a large company with a large advertising budget, rather than the informal entrepreneur you are. Remember that your mailer must reflect your personality; it must build an alliance with your customer, and therefore it must be a format that they can identify with and that you can continue to produce. Color brochures can put a big dent in your bank account—they are expensive to produce.

There are color-repro machines available that work like the familiar photo copy machine and are far less expensive than the four-color-process of printing.

One such copier is from Konica Business Machines. It is called the "Color 7" copier, and promises "true full color brilliance and contrast comparable to that of the original." The Color 7 can copy onto 8½" X 11", 11" x 14", and 11" x 17". You will find it available at Konica dealers and direct branch sales offices as well as quick print or copy centers since early 1987.

Color photocopies are not economical for a large newsletter run, but great fun for the family Christmas Letter!

Brochures can be made effectively on a copy machine with black and white photos and/or other artwork (see Chapter Five). Like pamphlets, the best size paper to use is 11"x17' folded in half to 8½" x 11", then folded again 3½" x 5½". You can use several 8½" x 11" shee and staple them together if you like.

If you are promoting yourself and your artwork, it is best to invest in a commercially printed brochure with halftoned or colored photos. Include photos of yourself and typical artwork. Because brochures can get outdated quickly, avoid printing fads or trendy samples of your work.

A R T I S T ' S   P O R T F O L I O

An artist's portfolio is generally kept in a loose leaf three ring binder, so material can be updated regularly. Include photos of yourself, your artwork, a resume', invitations to exhibits, good reviews, and other articles and write ups you have saved.

For a neater look, you can paste up the clippings and photos onto a single page and photo copy that. Keep your portfolio current, removing old artwork and inserting current works. You may include an actual original sample of drawings and watercolors if you like. A good book on the subject is "Promoting and Selling Your Art," by Carole Katchen (Watson-Guptill Publications, New York).

N E W S L E T T E R S

Newsletters can be from one to several pages and are mailed on a regular basis—quarterly, monthly, etc. The style is informal with condensed information or "news" worth keeping. It should not be entirely sales or promotional in nature. Because of its informative content, a newsletter may often be saved and/or passed on to others to read, thus increasing your readership and exposure.

A newsletter can be printed on 8½"x11", 8½"x14", or 11"x17".

PRICE LISTS

A price list is a listing of goods or services and the prices thereof. It may have wholesale as well as retail prices, and may include some photos or drawings. It is a very plain typed listing, in logical order, of goods or services for sale and a brief description of each. Include an order blank—make it easy for your customer to buy from you. And state when prices expire.

Very often price lists are included as a supplement to an expensive catalog that is printed without prices. The price list can then be updated as needed.

$ $ $ $ ¢ ¢ ¢ ¢

CATALOGS

Catalogs are more detailed than price lists and are most successfully issued by people already in business, to complement or extend that business. The term "catalog" infers photos and drawings of goods, detailed descriptions, prices, and order blanks. Stress the benefit to the customer as in all promotional writing! Catalogs are various sizes, 11"x17" folded to 8½"x11", or 8½"x11" folded to 8½"x5½" and stapled in the fold (saddle stitched). If you prefer, make a separate listing of prices, shipping fees, and expiration date. Although catalogs are most commonly printed professionally, you can make an effective one using a copy machine.

Consider using colored paper or cover stock for the cover of your catalog if you won't be using colored photos. A good book on catalogs is "How to Create Successful Catalogs" published by Sroge Publishing.

PRESS   RELEASE

A press release, also called a news release, is a single page of newsworthy information; a brief paragraph or two including all details, sent to radio, newspapers, etc., for "free" exposure. A press release has a certain form, should always be typewritten, and must include a contact person name and phone number.

Some newsworthy events that might land you coverage are: promotions in your business, teaching a class, volunteering, expanding your business, donations, and contributions. You will read more on press releases in Chapter Four.

BUSINESS   CARDS

It's been said you should give away 2000 business cards every month to be successful. I say it depends on what type of business you're in.

For service type businesses, like hair dressers and beauty consultants, give the cards. For retailers of gift wares, maybe a brochure or catalog would do more good. In any case, the design of your card—and you will have occasion to hand them out—should be simple and clean.

It should clearly state what goods or services you offer, and how you can be reached. Business cards show that you are sincere about your business, so they should look professional.

The standard business card size is 2"x3½" and you can have them printed at a print shop or make your own on card stock at the copy center. They can also be ordered through the mail economically. NEBS is one good source for business supplies.

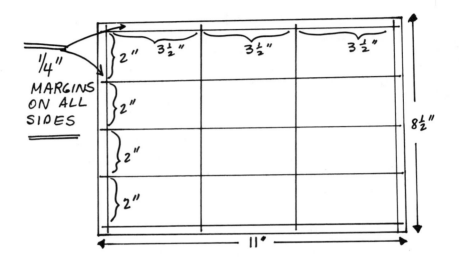

BUSINESS CARD LAYOUT

1. Use 8½"x11" white paper.
2. With non-repro pen, mark a ¼" margin on all four sides.
3. Using the inside margin lines, divide the 11" side into three equal sections (about 3½" each).
4. Divide the 8" side into four equal sections (about 2" each).
5. Pasteup design, logo, and other information in each section.
6. Photo copy onto card stock. Cut apart.

L E T T E R H E A D

Letterhead, or business stationery, also indicates your sincerity about your business, and can be made at the quick print shop or ordered from local printers or mail order suppliers.

Get standard size, 8½"x11", 20 pound paper. I prefer crisp white paper with a 25% cotton fiber content (it photo copies better). Don't use erasable paper, as it tends to smear when handled.

E N V E L O P E S

Standard business-size envelopes measure 4 1/8"x 9 1/2", and are called "number 10." They can be purchased at discount stationery stores and printed at your local printers, or ordered from stationery supply catalogs or local quick print shops. If you're on a budget, one way to get envelopes is to watch for coupon sales at your variety or drug store, and invest in a rubber return-address stamp and ink pad.

Using envelopes to mail promotional material does add to the cost of that material; however, if it is returned undeliverable, you can remove the promo-material from the envelope and use it again. There is also the opinion that hand addressed envelopes receive more immediate attention than folded and addressed mailers.

Envelopes come white and colored. Just stick to whatever you start with. I know a woman who uses only pink—when I see that pink envelope in my mail, right away I know who it's from and hurry to open it.

C O L O R !

Color sells. People like color! A mailer printed on colored paper will bring more response than one printed on white.

The most legible choice is black ink on yellow paper. Your copy center will have a variety of colored paper available, for about a cent more than plain white. Samples are posted on the wall, but ask to see a fresh sample of the color you want, as wall-displays can be faded from the daylight.

The copy center will print with black only. (There is one in my area that uses colored toner or ink—different colors on different days. Green ink on Mondays, blue on Tuesdays, etc). For colored inks you will need to find a print shop, as a rule.

Some of the most legible combinations of ink on paper are, in descending order of legibility: black ink on yellow paper, green ink on white paper, blue ink on white paper, white ink on blue paper, black ink on white paper. My first choice would be black ink on a pastel yellow paper, followed by black ink on most any other pastel paper.

The aim is consistency in your mailings, and it stands to reason that they should be as legible as possible. If your product, store, or service has a particular color connected to it, like pink to a certain line of cosmetics, then by all means use that color paper. But stick with black ink, and keep your layout (Chapter Six) clean and consistent—month after month.

P E R S O N A L   L E T T E R

You might wish to use a personal letter format. This works well for informal contact

such as person-to-person selling. Personal
letters may be handwritten or typewritten,
and should be signed.

WHAT CAN YOU STICK WITH?

Choosing a format that you can stick
with means choosing ink and papers you can
afford and obtain time after time. It
means choosing a layout design (Chapter Six)
that has your mandatory information in the
same place, time after time.

It means choosing a color you can live
with, and that will be available to you,
time after time.

Get samples of the papers you are con-
sidering. You may have to pay a small fee,
but you can take the colors home with you
and study them at length before making your
permanent choice. Once that decision is made,
you can rush your mechanical into the copy
center and place your order without hesitation, time after time.

If they should be out of your "color" at
press time, rest assured that the world will
not fall apart if you use a different color
now and again!

O T H E R   G O O D   S T U F F

In addition to using format and the copy
machine to build your business, you can use
the copy machine for fun. The "other good
stuff" you can make using the hints in this
book is limited only by your imagination.

Here are a few ideas to get your creative mind working:

ANNOUNCEMENTS—for weddings and anni-
versaries. Include photos and use hand
lettering.

BULLETINS—for inter-office notices; use comic letterheads or add clip art.

REPORTS—of clubs and organizations to members; single page or multi; include advertising.

CHRISTMAS LETTERS—to family and friends; include photos and holiday clip art with your yearly letter.

COOK BOOKS—for family, club, or church fund raiser; print; saddle stitch; use clip art and/or photos.

FAMILY HISTORIES—make a booklet recording the history of a favorite relative or make a family tree; include photos and spaces for new arrivals; make a copy for each family member.

MENUS—for the restaurant or special home entertaining; hand letter or print; add clip art; copy onto colored card stock; or use parchment or other special paper.

CLUB ROSTERS—for bridge club or RV club; include photos of meeting, outing, members.

PROGRAMS—for school or church; private dinner and award banquets.

POSTERS—for lost or found animals, for "garage sales," or directions to the picnic.

INVITATIONS—to birthday parties, anniversary parties, bridal showers, open house, grand opening of a business.

SCHOOL & FAMILY REUNIONS—invite members, then mail out a recap of the event complete with photos.

POETRY COLLECTION—now is the time to gather all of Aunt Mary's wonderful whimsical poetry, together with a few poignant photos, and produce a little booklet for family and friends. What a great tribute!

The things you can design and print are limited only by your imagination.

THINK ABOUT IT!

S U M M A R Y

1. Study the descriptions of various mailers.

2. Choose the format best suited to your needs, and one you can stick with. It's o.k. to change your mind!

3. Study information on choice of colored papers and inks. Choose one you can stay with.

4. Obtain blank papers of size and color you want to use. These may be purchased or received as samples from your copy center or printer.

5. Use your imagination to make "other good stuff" with the information you'll learn in this book.

3 Planning Promotions

An occasional immediate flyer will do nicely for your church picnic or a fund raising bake sale; but for a small business the "rule" is to promote at LEAST four times per year. Promotion serves four basic functions:

1. To increase sales
2. To generate interest in your product or service to new customers
3. To introduce a new product or service
4. To build familiarity with your present customers

In-store promotions run the gamut of everything from skin care clinics and scarf tying seminars to knitting machine demonstrations and the like. It is anything that shows off your product to customers while offering them a benefit at the same time.

Perhaps the most difficult part is getting customers to come to the promotion, to get them in the habit of coming to your business, and that is where your "promotional mailer" comes in.

"Direct mail is one of the least understood but most valuable forms of advertising available to the retailer. When used wisely it can help you increase your sales volume, bring in new customers to your store, and introduce new products or services. But when mailed out indiscriminately, without proper planning, it can cost you dearly." This is the wise advice of Dana K. Cassell from her book "How to Advertise and Promote Your Retail Store" (American Management Associations, New York).

The key to effective promotional mailings is planning. Or scheduling. Or goal setting. Whatever you want to call it. Timing is important, and the best day of the week for your mailer to arrive is Wednesday (EXCEPT for the Wednesday before Thanksgiving Day). Monday is too early for your shopper to make plans, and Friday is too late. Wednesday is perfect.

There are outside influences to be considered as well when planning your promotion.

OUTSIDE INFLUENCES TO PROMOTION

PAYDAYS. When do your customers get paid? What are the paydays of large employers in your area?

EVENTS. Community festivals, sports contests, big TV shows all work two ways: some will bring customers out into shopping areas; others will keep them home.

WEATHER. Like community events, the weather can affect your customer's shopping habits; it can also affect what product you sell or promote. Don't push charcoal briquets in the middle of monsoon season!

COMPETITION. You hear it often, "competition is good for business." You may not agree, but there is something you can get out of it when your competitor puts on a big promotion. It's called "piggybacking."

P I G G Y B A C K

Piggyback means to "ride" on the back of someone else's advertising or promotion. It also means you have to have knowledge of what's happening—by reading the television listings, signing up on your competitor's mailing list, and insisting that your manufacturer advise you in advance of national promotions.

Another way to be current is to read the newspapers. If your product or service fits in with a hot topic, promote it! That is the advantage of controlling your own material, you can have it printed and mailed in time to benefit from compatible events and promotions.

For example, if you learn that a well known color consultant will be on a morning television show, and you do color consulting yourself, whip out a flyer, mail it, post it, hand it out. Encourage folks to watch the show, then call you for an appointment! Be sure you have supplies on hand, and time to book colorings.

CONSUMER SPENDING HABITS

Consumers are creatures of habit. They tend to buy the same goods, frequent the same stores, and shop at the same times of the year. Some months bring much higher dollar sales than others and your promotion should be targeted to them. According to a Federal Reserve study, here are the trends in consumer spending, from the month of highest spending to the month of least spending: December, November, October, September/May, April, June, August, March, January/July, and February.

It would make sense to mail your promotional material prior to heavy spending months, wouldn't it? For mail order, however, the best months are January, February, October, August, November and September, according to the Direct Marketing Association.

HOW OFTEN TO MAIL?

Frequency of mailings depends on your type of business, but it's said that it takes at least three times for direct mail or advertising to get a potential consumer familiar with your name. Doctors may only need to send yearly reminders, where a beauty salon may want to notify clients every six weeks. A lot of small retail shops mail monthly. You should mail at least four times a year to maintain consumer awareness of your business. Popular mailing times are prior to Christmas, Mothers Day, back-to-school, and during the summer; however, let your product or service determine what four times of the year would serve you best. There are times NOT to mail, as well:

DO NOT MAIL before a holiday weekend when everyone is out of town or glued to a television football game.

DO NOT MAIL if it will not be delivered in time to take advantage of your offer.

Be aware of holiday traps—people shop on holidays, but mail doesn't move on holidays. To figure out the best day to mail, you will want to use a calendar.

USING THE CALENDAR

By now you are aware that a calendar will be important in planning your promotions. Get one with large areas for writing, such as an 8½"x 11" with a full month on each page.

A large poster-type that shows the entire year can be of great help. Hang it on the wall where you can see it daily, and use Postit Notes to mark coming events or ideas you'll want to follow up on.

You can make a simple year-at-a-glance calendar by folding an 8½"x11" piece of paper into thirds, as if to be stuffed into a business envelope, then fold it in half the other direction, and in half again. Open the paper, and you have twelve rectangles that can be outlined and labeled with the twelve months of the year. Start labeling with the current month and continue consecutively for a full year.

HOW TO MAKE A
YEAR-AT-A-GLANCE
CALENDAR

1. 8½ x 11.

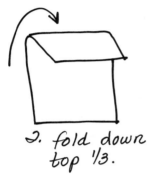

2. fold down top ⅓.

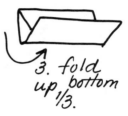

3. fold up bottom ⅓.

4. fold in half opposite way.

5. fold in half again

6. open. label each square with month of year.

This will be your Promotion Schedule for the next twelve months. Here are some occasions to note on your schedule (in pencil).

JANUARY. New Year's Day, Martin Luther King, Jr., Day.

FEBRUARY. Lincoln's Birthday, Washington's Birthday, President's Day. Valentine's Day.

MARCH. St.Patrick's Day, Palm Sunday (variable), Passover (variable), Easter Sunday (variable).

APRIL. April Fools Day (May also contain Passover, Palm Sunday, Easter Sunday—check a current commercial calendar).

MAY. Mother's Day, Armed Forces Day, Victoria Day (Canada), Memorial Day.

JUNE. Flag Day, Father's Day.

JULY. Independence Day (4th of July).

AUGUST. Create your own, keeping in mind that many people are out of town on vacation—which means that vacationers may be in your town from elsewhere!

SEPTEMBER. Labor Day, Rosh Hashanah (variable), Weddings.

OCTOBER. Columbus Day, Thanksgiving Day (Canada), United Nations Day, Halloween.

NOVEMBER. Election Day, Veterans Day, Thanksgiving Day. Note: the day after Thanksgiving is the biggest shopping day of the year in the USA.

DECEMBER. Hanukkah (variable), Christmas Day (with its day-after sales), New Year's Eve.

With your Promotion Schedule (calendar) at hand, read through the list again, noting holidays and occasions that would tie in with your product or service. Christmas is the biggest season in terms of retailing, with the day after Thanksgiving Day being the biggest shopping day of the year.

Does that mean you should spend your advertising money all for the Christmas season? Some retailers believe so. Others believe in spreading it out over the entire year, building familiarity. When the Christmas season comes, their customers will already be in the habit of visiting their businesses.

Other occasions you might be able to build a promotion around are Mother's Day (flowers, cards), back-to-school (clothing, shoes, paper and pencils), weddings (bridal wear, housewares), Easter (candy, flowers, spring apparel), Valentine's Day (flowers, cards, jewelry, candy), birthdays, graduations, new babies. The list of possibilities goes on; you get the idea!

Perhaps your product or service would do better on a seasonal basis—Winter, Spring, Summer, and Fall. Winter might be car care, firewood, catering or housecleaning services; Spring might emphasize cleaning and cleaning-products or yard maintenance; Summer might mean travel, or skin care, or roofing and repairs; Fall could be piano lessons, school clothes and supplies, or fitness and diet programs.

For example, a florist's four promotions might be built around Valentine's Day, Mother's Day, Weddings (September is very popular now) and Christmas.

After listing all the occasions that could relate to your product or service,

go back through your Promotion Schedule
and eliminate all but four, beginning with
the one most likely to bring the LEAST response!

To do that, you must understand your
product and your people.

YOUR PRODUCT, YOUR PEOPLE

Both product and people govern how and
when you promote. First you must know your
customer or potential customer: Who wants
or needs your product? Why? What would
motivate them to get it from you? What
is their gender, age, and income? Where are
you likely to find them? The chapter on
mailing can help you find the answers.

One of the easiest ways to determine
your customer's needs is to visualize yourself in his place. What would appeal to
you? What would you like to read about
your product?

And what about your product? It must
be the "right" item—something the consumer
needs—at the "right" price—one the consumer
will pay! Is your product obsolete? Maybe
you should sell it cheap, take your loss, or
call a liquidating company? Is it a year-
round commodity? Is it a brand new product
or service? Do you have sufficient supply
on hand? The answers to these questions
about your product and your people will
help you decide what to put into your mailer.

TOO MUCH TO REMEMBER?

It's true there is a lot to consider in
planning a promotion and mailer. That is

why this book is broken up into lists and
sections for easy reference.

Successful mailers don't just happen.
They are carefully planned. WITH PURPOSE!

SUMMARY

1. Purposes of a promotional mailer:
   to increase sales
   to generate interest of new customers
   to introduce a new product or service
   to build familiarity with customers

2. Outside influences to consider when
   planning: paydays, events, weather,
   piggyback opportunities

3. Consumer spending habits: most spending
   done in December, followed by November,
   October, Setpember/May, April, June,
   August, March, January/July, with
   February the lowest.

4. Promotion Schedule (calendar):
   Target holidays, special dates on your
   schedule that connect with your product
   or service. Start with four per year.

5. Know your product and your people.
   Target your mailers to the audience
   most likely to respond.

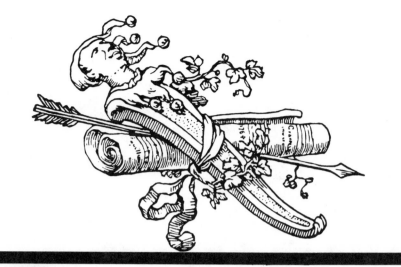

4 Writing Copy

To write good copy, you must first know what it is. Copy is the text, or words, put on paper to describe or explain your product or service and motivate the reader to buy it.

Copy fits into the spaces around your artwork. It is the words that motivate the reader to act upon your offer. It is persuasive writing. It must always provide a benefit to the customer, and must be "packed with punch." The Small Business Administration, in its pamphlet "Advertising Guidelines for Small Retail Firms," offers these tips for writing copy:

"Make your ads easy to recognize. Give your copy and layout a consistent personality and style.
"Use a simple layout. Your layout should lead the reader's eye easily through the message from the art and headline to

the copy and price to the signature.

"Use dominant illustrations. Show the featured merchandise in dominant illustrations. Whenever possible, show the product in use.

"Show the benefit to the reader. Prospective customers want to know 'what's in it for me.' But, do not try to pack the ad with reasons to buy—give the customers one primary reason, then back it up with one or two secondary reasons.

"Feature the 'right' item. Select an item that is wanted, timely, stocked in depth, and typical of your store. Specify branded merchandise and take advantage of advertising allowances and cooperative advertising whenever you can.

"State a price or range of prices. Don't be afraid to quote high prices. If the price is low, support it with statements which create belief, such as clearance or special purchase.

"Include store name and address. Double check every ad to make sure it contains store name, address, telephone number, and store hours."

You learned in Chapter One to put your name, address, telephone, and business hours on ALL promotional material. In Chapter Two you selected a format for your mailers, a "look" that will be recognized as "yours," month after month. To offer the

"right" item and price was discussed in Chapter Three, and throughout the book you'll encounter the first rule of promotional writing: to stress the benefit to the customer!

You'll learn about layout and illustrations in Chapter Six, so now we'll talk about actually putting your words, or copy, onto that blank piece of paper.

Writing copy can be divided into two segments, content and mechanics. The content means what types of things to write about and why, and the mechanics means sentences and words, and why and how they are used.

THE CONTENT OF PROMOTIONAL WRITING

Whether you are writing a flyer with few words or a newsletter with many, there are basic similarities in writing promotional copy.

All promotional writing has some common goals: to keep your name before the public; to change present consumer habits into ones of visiting your store or using your service or product; to create an acquaintance or familiarity with the reader. It should develop integrity for your business while stressing you personally, for in essence you are selling yourself.

If you are writing for a church or club, stress the organization. Let the reader get to know it as a friend. People like to do business with friends. People like to read about people.

Here are some questions and answers about content:

"How can I build integrity or credibility for my business with a mailer?"
Don't lie. If your product or service is "different," people will want to know

why. What makes it so? Tell them. If
your product or service is better, tell
them why and what it means to them, in
terms of benefit. Back up the statements made in your mailer with service and
dependability.

*"How can I compete with the large
chain stores?"*
Use your mailers to build an alliance
with your future customers. Stress what
you ARE and what you OFFER rather than
defending yourself against the larger
chain or discount store.
Let them know what you offer that your
competitors cannot. It may be service,
like color analysis, alterations, or infinite knowledge that only years of experience can bring. Accomodating business
hours, like evening, weekend, or early
morning appointments can make the difference
between the reader who calls you and the
reader who just as soon keep to his old
spending habits.
Keep your phrases positive and in good
taste. Not only does name calling leave
a bad taste with your reader, it could
lead to litigation. Check with your
attorney.

*"How can I make a newsletter informal
and friendly—include jokes?"*
A word of caution: it is great to be
friendly, but don't try to be cute. Many
consumers have no sense of humor at all,
and to be humorous, or try to be, is risky
at best. What is funny to one is offensive
to another. Play it safe; play it like a
business. Write like you would to a friend,
but leave the jokes to the commedians.

*"How can I get customers to read my
mailers?"*
Include something interesting! Not
only the benefit to the reader, but include
household hints, sewing tips, or a new

recipe. When readers learn to "expect" the little free morsels in your mailer, not only will they digest every word, but you'll find they share them with friends.

I know the owners of a kitchen shop who do newsletters monthly. They include not only a great recipe, but "hide" the monthly discount within the copy of the newsletter. Readers must take in every sentence to find the "secret word" that will give them a ten to forty percent discount!

In the newsletters I sent for my ladies' apparel shop, I included tips on clothing care and makeup. Not only were the news- letters anticipated, read, and shared, but women came into the shop to "sign up" for them!

"I've got a lot of 'right' items to sell, how can I promote them all in one mailer?"
Offering more than one item per mailer (or per page in a newsletter) is a little like trying to offer humor—not everyone understands it! But if you must, for cash flow reasons, then send a flyer with nothing but coupons on it, one for each item. The expiration and sale dates can vary for each coupon, which sometimes brings the reader into your store multiple times. And that helps to establish new shopping habits!

"How do I write a coupon?"
Coupons come in all shapes and sizes. Outline a coupon with some sort of border, and the reader's eye is immediately drawn to it.

Like all promotional writing, your cou- pon must be of value to the customer. It must be for a specified length of time, and the expiration date must be shown. State clearly any conditions or restrictions that apply to the use of the coupon. Some in- dicate "limited to stock on hand," while others say "not good on sale items," or "not redeemable for cash." In some states a cash value is required on all coupons, like "cash value 1/20 of one cent."

Show your business name, location, phone, and hours on the face of the coupon as well. A good exercise is to study coupons in newspapers and magazines that appeal to you. Why did they? What caught your eye? Use the same tactics when writing yours.

"I'd like to do a newsletter, but how can I make my products newsworthy?"
Relate your product or service to some currently newsworthy happening. Watch for public figures or situations that your readers are likely to recognize and respect.

For example, if the President's wife is seen in a beautiful new green suit by a specific designer—it's time to let your clients know you have it in stock or can order it for them.

If the local airstrip is having an air show the day of your church picnic, let readers know they can see the airplanes from the picnic site (which you carefully selected months ago).

If you're an artist, and a record-setting art auction is featured on the evening news, let your clients know about it while reminding them that you have original works available and, perhaps, currently on exhibit.

"How do I write a press release?"
Follow the format, use a typewriter, include pertinent information, know when to mail it and to whom and etc. There is much to consider when sending them, and you'll find a complete segment on press releases later in this chapter.

THE MECHANICS OF PROMOTIONAL WRITING

The mechanics of promotional writing could also be called the technical side of promotional writing, and include such things as nouns, verbs, adjectives, adverbs, headings, hook, bridge, body, close, and the way they work together.

If English grammar is not your best subject, don't let that stop you from writing your mailer. It is perhaps secondary to the main objective: getting your message across! If, however, you want to improve your grammar skills, there are a couple of things you can do. Get a dictionary. A paperback variety ($4 at the corner drug store) with about 50,000 words should do the job.

A dictionary will help you with many aspects of writing. You can find correct spelling, whether the word you want to use is a noun, verb, adjective or adverb, and of course if it portrays the meaning you intend.

When writing copy, you want to CHECK YOUR SPELLING, USE STRONG NOUNS (the name of a person, place, or thing), and USE STRONG VERBS (the word that shows action), rather than overusing adjectives (a word that describes or modifies a noun). Avoid using adverbs (words that describe or modify verbs, adjectives, or other adverbs) whenever you can. Adverbs usually end in -ly.

How can this copy be made better?

"A weak man will look great after using our Mighty-Muscle exercise appliance."

You can change the noun and its adjective "a weak man" to a stronger noun by using a name and thereby creating a picture in the reader's mind. The sentence can be shortened, if you plan to use an illustration or photo of the appliance.

"Hercules probably used the Mighty-Muscle!"

That's better, but the adverb "probably" tends to bring a feeling of doubt or negativity into the phrase, so rewrite the sentence again, bringing the reader into the action by asking a question:

"Did Hercules use the Mighty-Muscle?"

Now the reader not only pictures the muscular Hercules but asks himself "what is a Mighty-Muscle?" He cannot answer the question without more information—so you give it to him. In one or two short paragraphs. You've got him "hooked!"

Write like you are sending a telegram, not composing an essay for a contest. Be concise and precise. To the point! Be personal, write to one person ("you") as if you were writing to a friend. Your purpose is to inform, not entertain.

When laboring over your grammar, remember it's more important to get your message across. If you pay too much attention to grammar, your "style," the way you personally use the language, may get lost in the struggle.

What's the answer? Write like you talk. It's that simple! Use direct, simple sentences.

QUESTIONS & ANSWERS ON MECHANICS

"Is there a formula for promotional writing?"
There is a kind of structure or formula you can follow. It consists of a heading or hook, plus a bridge, a body, and a close. The HEADING, in large letters, should be your main customer benefit, followed by the BRIDGE, which links the heading to the body of your copy. The BODY sells your product or service, and the CLOSE or CALL-TO-ACTION motivates the reader to take you up on your offer.

"How do I motivate a reader to take me up on my offer?"
You ask. That may be by limiting the

offer to a specific number of days, such as a coupon. Higher priced items should be given more time than lesser priced ones, so that the reader can save up the money.

You may urge them to action by announcing that the supply or size is limited, or by giving away a free sample or door prize for a limited time.

"What is a hook?"

A hook is a heading or statement that piques the reader's curiosity. It should state the theme of the writing, what it is going to be about, what the benefit is to the reader. Think of it as bait on the hook, and you want a bite!

"What is a bridge?"

A bridge is a statement that follows the hook or heading, and leads the reader into the body of the copy. This leading from one statement to another is also called a transition, and should be smooth.

"If the headline draws the reader's eye, how can I get him to read the body?"

There are other eye catching devices you can use for that second glance.

<u>Underlining</u> can be effective. The caution is to NOT overuse it or it can become an irritation rather than eye catching. Be consistant in what is underlined, like headings, important benefits, catagories, or products. It's a good substitute for bold face type. (Type that is heavier than normal type).

Some insist that a postscript, a "<u>P.S.</u>" added to the bottom of a flyer or newsletter brings better results. You'll notice it on mailers you receive from magazines and book club offers and especially from big companies like those promoting sweepstakes contests. If you plan to use bulk mail (see Chapter Nine) the P.S. must be added to your original copy so that all mailers are exactly the same.

Words like <u>sex</u>, <u>love</u>, and familiar names will draw the reader's eye. Or appeal to the universal sense of greed—entice the reader to <u>save money</u>, <u>earn money</u>, <u>win money</u>, or generally "get something for nothing" and you'll get his attention.

Make people want your product or service in addition to their need, but keep comparisons to pleasant things. Some good words to use are <u>profit</u>, <u>achievement</u>, <u>success</u>, and <u>self esteem</u>, coupled with specific information.

"I can't seem to get started! What shall I do?"

It may help to inspire you by studying newspaper and magazine ads. Find the hook, the bridge, the body and the close or call-to-action. Can you spot the benefit? Is there more than one? Are there some ads you are more likely to respond to than others? Why? Chances are your customers will respond to ads the same way you do.

After you have looked over several ads for inspiration, it's time to once again grab a pencil and paper.

WRITING THE FIRST DRAFT

Here's what you do with your newfound inspiration and pencil and paper:

1. Pencil-in the words "heading" or "hook" in the upper left corner of your paper.

2. Skip down two or three inches, and pencil-in the word "bridge."

3. Skip down another two to three inches and pencil-in the word "body."

4. Skip down several more inches toward the bottom of the page and pencil-in, leaving two or three inches below it, the word "close" or "call-to-action."

5. Across the very bottom of the paper, pencil-in the words "name, address, phone, hours." Now you have started your first draft!

```
┌─────────────────────────┐
│  HEADING                │
│                         │
│  BRIDGE                 │
│                         │
│  BODY                   │
│                         │
│                         │
│  CLOSE                  │
│                         │
│  NAME + ADDRESS         │
└─────────────────────────┘
```

Return to the space marked "heading" or "hook" and pencil-in your customer benefit. To find that, put yourself in the customer's place and ask "what's in it for me?" It may be savings, service, or a unique item that only you stock.

Next, jump down to the space labeled "body." Pencil in the details of what you're offering, sizes, colors, usefulness, date, time, and anything else you think the customer will need to know.

Now that your brain is on a roll, write down under "close" the reason that customers will have to act fast. That may be an expiration date on the offer; the threat of a limited supply, a first-come first-served basis, moving or going out of business and so on. Ask yourself "If I read my ad, what would make me take advantage of it?"

Then back to the bridge. What will connect your heading or hook to the body? Of course it depends on your particular situation and merchandise.

Here again you can study the mailers you

receive, as examples are often the best teachers.

Consider the plight of Wally Bygolly. He has a bakery, and his specialty is cakes. Decorated cakes. For the last two years, Wally's sales have been going down, largely due to a discount supermarket on the out-skirts of town that has an in-house bakery. Wally has a problem.

He grabs a pencil and paper and makes his worksheet:

Problem: need more sales

Solutions: 1. cake sale
2. promotion, give away cake
3. promotion on wedding cakes
4. give in to competition,
layoff help; maybe close

Wally starts eliminating his solutions. Scratch 1, he is already losing money, a sale on cakes would only lose him more.

Scratch 2, he's tired of the free-loaders—people who come for a free cake and never come back. He wants to build an alliance with his customers and get repeat business. He must do something that will benefit them more than a free cake.

Scratch 4, Wally has been in business for twelve years. He will not quit without a fight!

That leaves 3, have a promotion on wedding cakes.

Because his Promotion Schedule (calendar) quickly shows that the big wedding season is three months away, Wally decides to pro-mote now by taking orders.

He chooses to make a flyer because it is fast, can be mailed as well as posted in his window and around town.

Without hesitation, Wally turns over his original worksheet and begins drafting his

copy. He knows that his promotional writing must (1) grab the reader's attention, (2) give a benefit to the reader, (3) state his shop name, location, phone, and business hours, (4) give credibility to his work, and (5) motivate the reader to act.
Here is his first draft:

HOOK: wedding cakes; anyone with a wedding in the near future will have an eye out for the perfect cake. Use photo/drawing.

BRIDGE: benefits to customer; order cake and not have to worry about it; get flowers on cake to match the wedding colors; offer a discount on cake ornaments ordered at the same time (additional sales)

BODY: must include why Wally's Cakes are special (fresh ingredients, custom designed, delivery and set up included, serve 10 to 500, give credibility to business—12 years) Wally is a home town boy done good!

CLOSE: motivate reader to act now. deadline, 3 weeks.

Wally knows his product, now he must consider his people. Who needs to see his flyers?
"It's the bride and her family that pay for the cake," he reasons, "so I must appeal to them. Most likely the mother."
A few rewrites later, Wally has the content for his flyer and will use clip art of a wedding cake. Artwork always grabs the eye, and anyone planning a wedding will most likely read the rest of the flyer.
Here's Wally's final promotional copy:

WEDDING CAKES

Does your daughter deserve the wedding cake of her dreams? Wally's Cakes has been supplying the stuff dreams are made of for over twelve years.

Our cakes are designed to your specifications, and baked with the finest fresh ingredients available. We can match your colors in luscious buttercream flowers on cakes that serve from an intimate gathering of ten to a gala of 500 or more. Free delivery and set up, too!

Order your wedding cake before May 27th and get a 40% savings on your choice of wedding cake ornament.

W A L L Y ' S   C A K E S

Corner of Promise & Lace   (555)123-4567
Open Monday-Saturday 9 to 6. Eves by appt.

An analysis of Wally's copy shows right away that "Wedding Cakes" is the heading. It reinforces the illustration, which is good. Many times you will wait until your copy is entirely written before deciding on the wording for the heading. It must be short, yet tell what you're offering.

The next sentence "does your daughter..." is the hook that grabs the reader's attention and immediately gets her involved with the copy. It appeals to emmotion—no mother or father would admit that their little girl didn't deserve a special cake for her wedding. The second sentence "Wally's Cakes..." is the bridge that links the hook to the body. It lets the reader know what this flyer is all about. It tells the reader three things very quickly with few words—the name of the shop and that Wally's can solve the reader's problem (supplying the stuff dreams are made of) with dependability (in business for twelve years).

Now comes the body of the writing, "Our cakes are..." which tells the details of size, colors, usefulness, and what benefit to the customer. In Wally's case, the reader knows that the cakes are specially designed, finest ingredients, buttercream flowers to match color scheme, and that the bakery will deliver and set up—what a load off her mind! The reader now realizes that she NEEDS this product and service.

The close "With any wedding cake..." repeats Wally's basic theme of wedding cakes and throws in a kicker to motivate the reader even more. Not only will she be saved the worry of where to get the cake and if it will tie in with the wedding colors, and who will deliver it, but also she can save 40% on the top ornament!

Wally has used the tried and true method of "urging the customer to act now." Always ask for an order or sale. Make it easy for the customer to buy from you.

Because weddings can be expensive, Wally has allowed a time limit of three weeks

on his 40% offer. He will also ask for a
50% deposit with the wedding cake order,
which will help his immediate cash flow
problem. Customers, new and old alike, will
be reminded of his wonderful birthday and
anniversary cakes while they are in his
bakery. He will also ask for names and
addresses for his mailing list when new
customers call or come into his shop.

WRITING THE FINAL DRAFT

You may need to write and rewrite your
copy many times, until you are satisfied
with it. Rather than rewrite the same paragraphs over or erase your worksheet until
there are holes in it, simply cut out those
paragraphs that you like and tape them onto
your next draft.

When your copy is ready for typesetting,
refer to Chapter Five. It's a good idea
to make your layout or "dummy" (Chapter Six)
before doing your typesetting, which is the
final typing or printing that will be pasted
on your mechanical.

PRESS RELEASE

What is a press release? It's a newsworthy bit of information sent to a newspaper or radio program in hopes of getting
mentioned at no charge, with the end result
of bringing attention to your business. It
is also called a "news release."
You can spot press releases in your

local paper by finding articles that mention
local businesses—events, promotions, new
locations or services offered, awards
received or an employee's retirement—all
are typical press release information. You
can believe that the newspaper "got wind" of
it because of a press release sent by the
business itself.

Press releases benefit both the newspaper (free news copy and hopes of securing
paid advertising at a later date), and the
business (free exposure to possible new
customers).

With a little creativity, you can turn
almost anything into a press release. A
few newsworthy reasons to send a press release
are: donation to a public institution or fund
raising drive, giving a workshop, class, lec-
ture, or starting a school, creating a new
recipe, inventing a helpful household
hint, writing a letter to the editor, or
donating instruction to a prison, nursing
home, or hospital. Carole Katchen gives
a lengthy list in her book *Promoting and
Selling Your Art* (Watson-Guptill Publications, 1978).

To whom is a press release mailed? To
determine where your best audience is—the
readers that would be likely to respond to
your news—study local newspapers for advertising and printed press releases. What
type of "news" are they likely to print?
What types of advertising do they accept?
What type of person reads that paper? The
advertising will tell you. Would those
readers be likely candidates for your product
or services? If so, then write down the
newspaper name, mailing address, and the
name of the editor in charge of the section
your press release would most likely appear
in. If you're sending news of a new auto-
mobile tire or a new line of tennis rac-
quets, aim for the sports section. Likewise,

if the paper uses a lot of cigarette ads, don't expect the editor to print your anti-smoking letter!

Another thing you can do is scan the Yellow Pages under Newspapers and Radio Stations for addresses and phone numbers of the ones you would like to contact. Then call each one, requesting the name of the person or managing editor in charge of your target section—the sports editor, or business and finance editor, or the women's editor and so on.

Ask also what the "closing" or "deadline" day is for the following week's paper. If it is a "daily" paper, forget the deadline and just mail it in (see "When should it be mailed?" later in this section.)

Any press release addressed to a specific editor, by name, must be mailed right away. There is a great turnover in editors in the publishing world, and if the one you addressed has moved on, your press release may be discarded without even opening the envelope!

Another place to find names of newspapers and magazines is *Writer's Market,* a listing of publishers printed yearly by Writer's Digest. You can find a current copy in the public library. Also in the library is *The Literary Market Place,* which lists papers and radio and television stations nationwide. It should be in the reference section; ask the librarian for help if you cannot find it.

When should a press release be mailed?
To know when to send a press release, you will have to understand "lead" time. That is the time a newspaper or magazine needs to review, edit, and typeset your press release before printing it in a particular issue. Your press release must be sent well ahead of time. Figure out mailing dates by using your Promotion Schedule (calendar).

For example, Mary Smith owns a dress

shop in which she also does color analysis and makeup by appointment. She has learned that a prominent color consultant will be on the local morning television show on Thursday, June 17th. She has a week and a half to piggyback a promotion to bring additional business. Here's what she pencils in on her worksheet:

PROBLEM: motivate new customers to color analysis
SOLUTION: piggyback on current tv show

FORMAT: flyer for window and community; press release to all three community papers

A quick look at her Promotion Schedule tells Mary that she must mail her press release no later than Tuesday, June 8th,, if it is to appear in the paper of Wednesday, June 16th—three days before her event. She calculated that by working <u>backwards</u> from the date of her piggyback promotion.

SATURDAY, June 19th: piggyback seminar on color. After lunch hour, after kids' matinee' begins at 2:00 pm
THURSDAY, June 17th: local television show with prominent color consultant; viewers get motivated to act
WEDNESDAY, June 16th: local papers delivered; some arrive Thursday because they are mailed; best issue for news to be in— too late to forget it, early enough to plan to attend.
MONDAY, June 14th: deadline for anything that is to appear in the paper of Wednesday, June 16th
WEDNESDAY, THURSDAY, FRIDAY, June 9, 10, 11: best days of the week for an editor to receive press releases; editors get too much mail on Monday and Tuesday; Wed-Thurs-Fri should allow sufficient time to consider/edit/typeset by the deadline.

TUESDAY, June 8th: mail press releases to local papers so they will arrive on Wednesday.

The preceding week (June 1st) may have been even better for mailing a press release, as Mary may have "lucked out" and had her news printed in two weekly issues; however, she knew of the TV booking only one and one half weeks in advance.

Because the local papers are small and hope for future paid advertising, Mary has a very good chance that her press release will be printed. She can also use the same wording to make flyers to post on her windows and community bulletin boards as well as hand out to passersby.

JUNE

S	M	T	W	Th	F	S
		1	2	3	4	5
6	7	8	9	10	11	12
13	14	15	16	17	18	19
20	21	22	23	24	25	26
27	28	29	30			

How many press releases to send? How many papers and radio programs in your area meet your requirements? Press releases are like good photographer's film—if you use a whole lot, some are bound to make good!

Be wary of sending to magazines. They may have lead times from three to six to twelve months, so they're not compatible with press releases from small businesses with an urgent need. They may be great for large companies with new products and a large advertising budget.

Must press releases be typewritten? In
a word—YES. See the sample that follows
in this section for form: headings, margins,
and spacing. One school of thought is
that each press release should be original
type; however, because you will be sending
several, a good, clean, clear copy from
today's photocopiers should work as well.

Use crisp, white, 8½"x11" paper, never
colored, and never erasable paper (it tends
to smear when handled by as many people
as your press release will be).

Letterhead, or company stationery, is
acceptable for press releases. There are
those who feel that the letterhead detracts
from the message of the press release and
those who feel it adds credibility. Leave
at least two inches below the actual letterhead to begin your press release.

I prefer plain, crisp, white paper,
20 pound, 25% cotton fiber, with the company
name and address typed below the name of the
contact person at the bottom.

Whichever you choose, use a clean, very
black ribbon (film or carbon ribbon is best,
but use what you have). Type on one side
only, double spaced. Keep abbreviations
to a minimum to avoid misunderstanding, and
write out single digit numbers, like "two"
rather than "2." Numerals may be used for
multiple digit numbers like "22," and for
dates "July 22, 1987" and for the time of
day "2:00 p.m." and for amounts of money
"$22.00."

You can enclose a reply card, postage
paid, asking if the press release will be
used and when, but don't push your luck!
They know what you're after, and at what
price.

Is there a "formula" for writing a
press release? There is a kind of a formula for writing press releases. Don't
write to tell them you are selling Bottled

Body Odor for $10.00 a bottle. That's an ad, and you must pay for it.

Just remember that you are writing a news or press release, so your (1) reason must be newsworthy, or seem that way. You will want to indicate a (2) benefit to the reader, to (3) create interest in your business and motivate readers to seek you out, which naturally means your (4) business name, location, and phone must be included. Mention any (5) unusual specifics about your product or services without becoming high-tech, and (6) include dates, times, and the cost to the reader.

It doesn't hurt to work in a (7) short biography of yourself; when the business was started; its goals and purpose (to benefit the customer, of course). Start with the most important "news" item first and decrease to the least important. That way, if the editor has limited space, the least important information is the most likely to be cut.

You must also give your name and phone number as a contact person, and indicate that you are available and willing to be questioned. This often leads to an interview.

What if they call me for an interview? Heaven forbid? Nonsense! An interview request as a result of your press release is icing on the cake.

Make an appointment, be polite at all times, have your notes ready—your name, how you got started in your business and why, what benefit you offer to customers with your product or services, and (it never hurts to try) any upcoming event that could benefit readers. Be cautious of saying things "off the record." It's best to NOT tell an interviewer anything you don't want to see in the paper!

Thank them for their time and interest and request a tear sheet of the article or story. A tear sheet is a torn-out page bearing your article that is taken from a printed issue of the newspaper.

Dress nicely, and have your hair and face presentable. You may just be photographed, too!

On the following page is a press release from Wally's Cakes.

Before reading the analysis that follows the sample press release, test yourself for being able to recognize the various "parts" of his press release, and what purpose they serve.

May 1, 1988

FOR IMMEDIATE RELEASE

Wally's Cakes on Promise Avenue at Lace Street will celebrate its 12th anniversary on Saturday, May 13th, with an open house from 2:00 to 4:00 p.m.

Samples of a new flavor in wedding cakes, orange-coconut, will be offered along with free coffee and a 40% savings on all orders for cake top ornaments.

Wally's also designs birthday and retirement cakes, but is especially known for wedding cakes with buttercream roses tinted to match the wedding flowers and attendants' dresses.

Wally studied at the Paris School of Pastrie' and served as dessert chef for Chicago Cakes before returning home to Arbortown, where he started Wally's Cakes.

FOR MORE INFORMATION CONTACT:

Wally Bygolly

Wally Bygolly
3323 Promise Avenue
Arbortown, USA 33323
(555) 123-4567

Let's analyze Wally's press release. In the very first sentence, he has (1) given the business name, location, (2) given credibility to his business by showing how long he's been there, (3) given the day and time of the event. The time limit, "from 2:00 to 4:00 p.m." will motivate readers to get there before 4:00 p.m.

Wally's second sentence gives the customer a benefit (free sample of cake and coffee) which also motivates. It also points out an unusual aspect of his business (a new flavor) and offers yet another benefit (40% savings) to the customer as well as lets them know what he does besides wedding cakes.

The third sentence expands on his capabilities and lets readers know his work is unique. Readers begin to visualize a cake that matches the color scheme of the wedding.

The last sentence is a "short bio." It gives Wally's qualifications and makes the reader identify with the "home town boy."

Recipients of the press release can easily contact Wally for more information, verification, or to request an interview because his full name, address, and phone number appear at the bottom as "contact person."

Wally has added an informal, personal touch by individually signing each press release.

S U M M A R Y

1. Copy is the writing, or text, that fits into the space around your illustrations or drawings or photos.

2. The common goal of all promotional material is to keep your name before the public.

3. Promotional writing is friendly, but NOT cute.

4. Formula for writing promotional copy is heading/hook + bridge + body + close.

5. Some tools to use in writing are underlining, postscripts, and handwritten notes prior to mailing.

6. A press release must be newsworthy, not simply advertising.

7. Addresses for newspaper and radio stations can be found in the Yellow Pages or in *The Literary Market Place* at your library.

8. Use a calendar to plan your mailings and events. Call it your PROMOTION SCHEDULE.

9. Be thankful for interviews; be polite; be well dressed; know your subject; don't say what you don't want repeated.

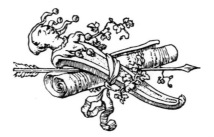

5 Photos, artwork, & type

Your camera ready pasteup (mechanical) will consist of photos, artwork, and type. Or some combination of each.

With a few graphic aids and some helpful hints, you can produce a respectable piece of promotional material on the photo copier.

PHOTOS

<u>Where to get photos?</u> If the manufacturer of your product doesn't provide camera ready artwork or black and white "glossies," you can take them yourself. A 35mm camera is nice, and any black and white film will do, but ask for glossy prints rather than the satin finish when having them developed.

Use a self-stick label on the back of your photos to record date, person, product, etc., for future use. It is best to <u>show your product in use.</u>

You can have someone take photos for you, but be certain to give them credit. Care must be taken to not infringe on copyrights when using other photographers' work. Get permission and give credit. One book covering that subject is *Law and the Writer,* edited by Kirk Polking and Leonard S. Meranus (Writer's Digest Books). This is not to suggest that any book can substitute for legal counsel. You should also get releases from people in your photos, and you can find a "model release" form in *Writer's Encyclopedia* edited by Kirk Polking (Writer's Digest Books).

<u>Halftones</u> are black and white photos in which the black and gray areas are broken up into a series of small dots to retain detail when printed. If you look at a magazine or newspaper photo with a magnifying glass, you will see the dots—large in dark areas and smaller in light areas. Halftones are required if you are going to have your mailer printed, and a print shop can make them for you from a glossy black and white photo.

You can get acceptable results from black and white photos on a plain paper copier by using the right graphic aid. And it's much less expensive than halftones.

<u>Use only black and white photos</u> for reproduction. A copy machine sees differently than the human eye, and reproduces reds and pinks as black, some blues as white, and greens and yellows as mud! Use sharp, glossy black and white prints, and cover them with a "copy screen" prior to photocopying (more information on copy screens later in this chapter).

<u>Crop (cut) your photo</u> to the desired size and content prior to pasteup. To crop a photo, simply cut off distracting backgrounds and things not pertaining to the subject. Make your corners square and sides parallel by using a triangle or ruler and marking cut lines. Cut with a scissors if you must, but an Xacto knife and metal ruler will do the best job. Always use a metal

ruler when cutting, never plastic or wood.
Reducing and enlarging photos is best
done under professional conditions and NOT
by photocopy machines. Use what size photo
you have, after cropping, and fit your copy
around that. Purchase a white "copy screen"
at the local graphic supply store or by mail
order from one of the suppliers listed in
the Appendix of this book. One source I
use repeatedly is Dot Pasteup Supply.

A copy screen is a clear film that has
been printed with white dots and comes in
65, 85, or 100-line (number of dots per
linear inch). The film can be self-adhesive
or not, and is simply placed over your black
and white photo before copying. An 85-line
screen gives good results on most plain paper
copiers. The more dots per inch, the finer
the detail. Quality books use a 120 to 150
line halftone on photos. Not all copiers
will bring good results with the finer
screens, and that is why the 85-line screen
is recommended. You can experiment with the
machine you will be using to find out which
works best for you. Copy screens cost $2
to $3 each for a 9"x12" size.

Dot halftone screens are available for
Polaroid cameras that use black and white
film (100 to 450 series). The screen in-
stalls into the film pack and makes "instant"
halftones. It is available from The Printers Shopper.

ARTWORK

Line drawings are one kind of artwork
you might want to use in your layout. They
can be drawn freehand or made on tracing
paper with a permanent ink marker. Lay the
tracing paper over a photograph or other
artwork and outline as desired, adding
detail and shading with short quick strokes.
Another method is to trace lines directly on
a black and white photo, then "fade" the image
on a copy machine until only the lines remain.
You will get best results from large

line drawings that have been reduced prior to pasteup. Reducing a drawing minimizes flaws, and can be done on most of today's copy machines with little effort.

Shading in line drawings can be effectively done using short strokes close together, or cross-hatching, or you can purchase shading film, which is also called "benday."

Shading film is similar to a copy screen, but the dots and shading patterns are black, and come in percentages from 10 to 70—the higher the percentage meaning the more dense the dots or pattern of shading. Shading film is self-adhesive and can be used over line drawings and clip art. You can also paint on shading film with white poster paint or correction fluid, or use white transfer letters for a "drop out" lettering effect.

Sometimes a 10% shading film will set off your letterhead or organization heading nicely from the rest of the information and make it easy to recognize. Try covering a "box" of supplemental information within your newsletter with light (10% or 20%) shading to separate it from the rest of the copy.

Four strokes to use for shading with pen & ink.

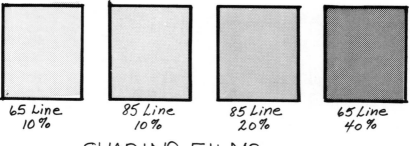

| 65 Line | 85 Line | 85 Line | 65 Line |
| 10% | 10% | 20% | 40% |

SHADING FILMS

White transfer lettering on 65 line, 40% shading film.

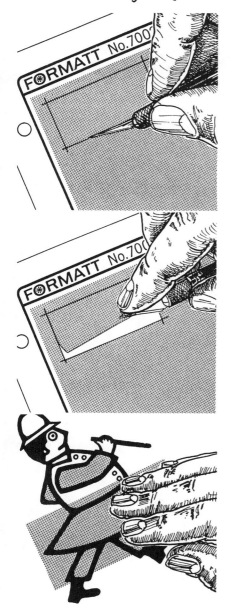

1. Cut out a section of shading film, slightly larger than area to be covered. Overlap all cut lines at each corner.

2. Turn knife and slide dull edge of blade under corner of film and lift off backing paper.

3. Lay shading over area to be covered and smooth lightly into place.

4. Cut lightly within the outline of the area to be shaded.

5. Peel away excess shading film.

6. Burnish the shading film firmly so it appears as if it was actually printed on the drawing.

Instructions courtesy of GRAPHIC PRODUCTS CORPORATION

Clip art is another type of artwork you can use. Black drawings and illustrations printed on a slick white paper that can be clipped out and used as needed for original pasteup is called clip art. The art depicts different seasons, professions, symbols, and the like. Letraset® makes clip art, and you can write to them for more information. Other sources are Graphic Products Corporation (available in most graphic supply stores), and The Printers Shopper and Dynamic Graphics. Creative Media Services offers a line of cartoon-type clip art custom designed to your needs.

Librarians can help you find sources of clip art, and often you can use artwork and headlines from newspapers and magazines (avoid using copyrighted work). You'll recall that red looks black to the photo copy machine, so artwork printed in red at Christmastime can also be used.

Clip art samples courtesy of The Printers Shopper

Clip art can be purchased on sheets similar to transfer lettering, and in collections or books like this one from Creative Media Services.

<u>Newspaper artwork</u> that is saved for a long period of time will tend to yellow and will be difficult to copy. Make yourself a photo copy on white paper while the clipping is fresh, and save that for a later date. The best newspaper and magazine clippings to use are very black print on shiny white paper.

<u>Charcoal</u> on rough paper is another

way to produce shaded drawings if you care to expose your artistic talent! Line drawing, shading film, clip art, and charcoal drawings do NOT require the use of a copy screen for reproduction.

<u>Reductions of line drawings and clip art</u> can be made on many brands of copiers. Ask your copy center assistant to show you how it's done, unless of course they do it for you! Reductions can be to 98%, 74%, 65% or smaller. Some of the new copiers have infinite settings for reduction work. If you need something very, very small, like art for a business card, think about reducing a reduction! A good rule of thumb for normal reductions is to limit reduction to 45% of the original (and limit enlargements to 150% of the original).

<u>Enlargements</u> of line drawings will magnify any errors or flaws, but will give you a good base for tracing a new original!

For filling in <u>large solid areas,</u> purchase what is called a <u>masking film</u> rather than filling in with pen and ink which tends to be uneven. Masking films come in red but photocopy black to produce a solid black area. Use a masking film with transfer letters that are white for a "drop out" print. (Light print on a black background).

A <u>light box</u> or <u>light table</u> will come in handy for preparing artwork and can be purchased at the local art or graphics supply store, college bookstore, and from The Printers Shopper, Dot Paste Up Supply, or Dick Blick.

— White transfer letters on masking film)

Blockout

A light box is not a necessary tool. You can use the popular solar powered infinite depth unit (also called a window), or make your own with a picture frame, a piece of plexiglass, some sticks, and a light.

A light box helps you see through the paper you're working on to the graph lines you have placed underneath. Use it when inking a drawing, adding shading material, positioning transfer letters, and when doing your final pasteup.

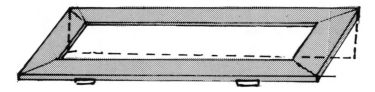

1. *Find a heavy, wide picture frame with a flat back. 12x16 or 16x20, inside dimensions, will do nicely. Look for them at garage sales or thrift stores.*
2. *Get a piece of plexiglass or frosted plate glass to fit the size frame you find.*
3. *Turn the frame back side up, add one long or two short supports to raise the frame to a 45° angle. Add stoppers on the front side to keep it from slipping forward.*

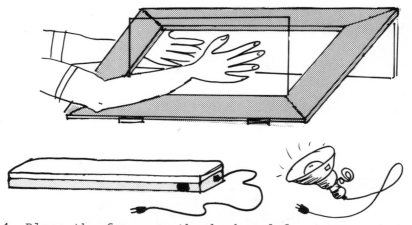

4. *Place the frame on the back and front supports, insert glass, and place a light behind it. An under-cabinet fluorescent light does a good job, and is cooler than the incandescent type.*

Tracing paper will allow you to do the same thing. Or you can rule guide lines directly onto your pasteup sheet with a non-repro pen or pencil, available at graphic supply shops or any of the suppliers mentioned in this book. Non-repro pens and pencils are light blue and do not reproduce when copied.

Dressing refers to borders and arrows and other symbols used to "dress up" your mechanical. They can be used to lead the reader's eye to a certain area, like a hand with one finger pointing, or to tie together your information, like a border. You can make your own border using a ruler and permanent ink marker, or you can purchase border tapes. The tapes can be solid or broken lines (good for coupons), or ornate designs. They are easy to apply.

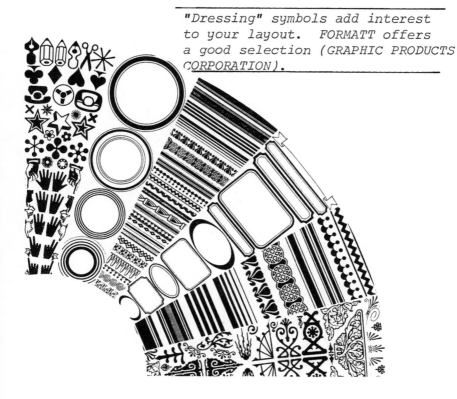

"Dressing" symbols add interest to your layout. FORMATT offers a good selection (GRAPHIC PRODUCTS CORPORATION).

TYPE

The copy in newspapers, magazines, and books is professionally typeset and is called "type." (This book was "typeset" with a typewriter and transfer lettering). Many desktop publishers can set type with a sophisticated computer system and laser printer. YOUR choices will be these: hand lettering, typewritten copy, transfer lettering, or a combination thereof. Transfer lettering is also referred to as instant lettering, dry transfer, or cold type.

Whichever you use, it must be very black, very clean, and applied in a straight line on crisp white paper. When you're ready to do your "typesetting," turn to Chapter Seven, PASTEUP AND SUPPLIES.

<u>Headings</u> are very effective when made with transfer lettering. Transfer lettering is available in "rub off" or "lift off" type. It comes in different "points" or sizes (height) and a wide range of styles. The sheets vary in size, and content, with some carrying only capital letters, some only lower case letters, some with numbers or symbols only and some a combination, so it must be selected with care.

<u>"Rub off" letters</u> are applied by placing the entire sheet of letters over your layout, then rubbing off each desired letter with a burnishing tool. I have been known to sometimes use an orange stick or a dried out ball point pen—not the choice of fine graphic artists, but it works for me!

One way to work with "rub off" lettering is to burnish them onto tracing paper (onto which you have drawn a base line with non-repro pen). The tracing paper may then be cut and the letters or heading positioned exactly as desired; this is especially helpful when centering a heading.

<u>"Lift Off" letters,</u> on the other hand, come on a self-adhesive film. Each letter is cut around, together with a section of the

guideline beneath it, and placed on the layout sheet. Before final burnishing, the fine guideline beneath the letters is trimmed away. Lift off lettering may also be first placed onto tracing paper for ease of centering, but a better way is to use a "Headline-Setter" such as Formatt offers. The Headline Setter is a gridded plastic strip on which the lift off acetate letters are placed, matching guidelines. The word or words can then be placed onto the layout and the guidelines trimmed away and removed before final burnishing.

Headings can also be made effectively using a calligraphy pen or felt tip pen. Newspaper and magazine headings often fill the need.

When <u>hand lettering or printing</u>, use permanent black ink, whether with a calligraphy pen or fine tip marker. Print on crisp white paper, using a gridded layout sheet underneath to keep your letters even. You can draw parallel lines with a non-repro pencil right on your lettering sheet if you prefer. You'll find tips for drawing parallel lines later in this chapter.

FORMATT offers a good selection of transfer lettering. (See your graphic arts store or the GRAPHIC PRODUCTS CORPORATION catalog.

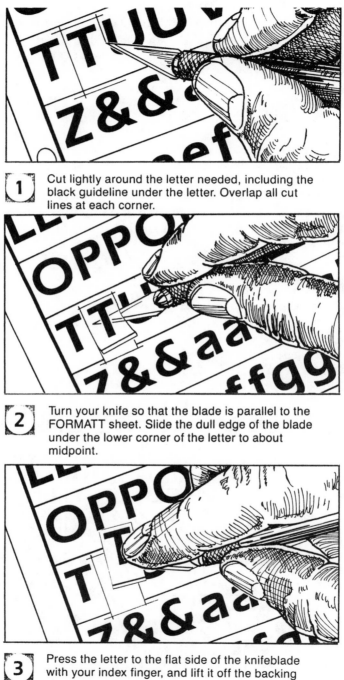

1 Cut lightly around the letter needed, including the black guideline under the letter. Overlap all cut lines at each corner.

2 Turn your knife so that the blade is parallel to the FORMATT sheet. Slide the dull edge of the blade under the lower corner of the letter to about midpoint.

3 Press the letter to the flat side of the knifeblade with your index finger, and lift it off the backing sheet.

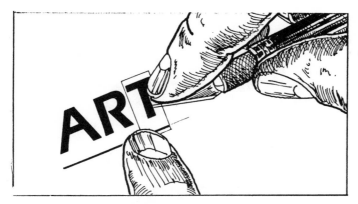

 4 Position and press the black guideline under the letter over a non-repro blue line already drawn on your art board or paper. Remove the knifeblade and smooth letter into place.

5 After your headline is completed, trim away and remove the black FORMATT letter guidelines.

6 Burnish firmly and thoroughly until all edges and overlaps disappear. The harder you burnish, the better your work will reproduce.

Some stationery and graphic supply stores have what is called a <u>lettering machine</u>. For a fee, you can have letters printed one at a time on a strip of clear acetate. These adhesive strips, or headlines, can then be applied to your final pasteup.

Typical lettering machine

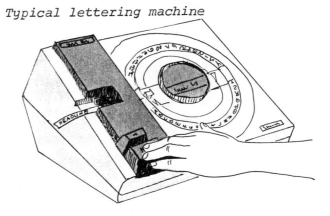

The <u>typewriter</u> can of course be used for headlines and copy. Headlines might be made in all upper case (capital) letters, while the copy is done in a combination of upper and lower. The ribbon must be black and the imprint clean for good reproduction. Carbon or film ribbon is of course preferred, but use what you have. Keys must be clean!

The more simple the type style, the easier it is to read. "Courier" typestyle, such as IBM provides, is one of the most popular. The type in this book was done on an Adler electric typewriter, and the basic typestyle is called "Isabelle."

Typewriters used to come with one of two type choices—"Pica," a larger type with ten characters to the inch, and "Elite," a little smaller, with twelve characters to the inch. Elite was used extensively for business correspondence although Pica was considered easier to read.

Today's typewriters have changeable type elements or wheels, which can add interest

to your mailer. Keep changes to a minimum—
perhaps using only two typestyles, one for
all of the copy, and another one for your
business name and location.

Combining transfer lettering and typewriter type gives a professional look to your
mailer. You can use transfer lettering to
make your business "logo" as well. Your
logo can be reduced on the photo copy machine
for use in designing your business cards.

Logo means the particular way your
business name is always seen. It can be a
certain style of type, or lettering, or be
combined into a graphic design that becomes
recognized easily by the public. You can
call it your business "emblem" or "signature"
and have it printed on all related business
forms, wrappings, and etc.

If you design your own logo, make it
large and then have it reduced to bring any
flaws to a minimum, and to have it take on
a professional appearance.

CHARTS & GRAPHS

To show a comparison of quantity, as
in sales figures or effectiveness between
brands, use a bar chart rather than a line
graph. Bar charts are better understood by
readers, although circle graphs are popular too. To further enhance or distin-
guish the bars or sections of circle,
add shading with pen and ink or shading films.

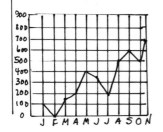

Line graph

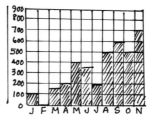

Bar graph

DRAWING LINES

You can use your <u>typewriter</u> to quickly draw parallel lines. Simply insert the paper, release both margins and move each to its extreme left and right. Set the line spacing for single or double—whichever you prefer. Hold a fine tip black marker (or a non-repro pen) into the hole or V-groove on the line finder that rests against the paper. Now use the carriage release to move the line finder across the page!

On an electric typewriter, move the line finder to the right margin, hold the pen tip in the hole or V-groove, and hit the return key.

For lines in the opposite direction, remove paper and insert it in the opposite direction.

MAKING LINES WITH
A TYPEWRITER

Hold marker in groove or hole in line-finder. Press firmly against paper. Use carriage release or return to move line across paper!

An easy way to divide a paper into
equal parts is by use of a <u>ruler</u>—but not in
the usual way!

Hold the ruler across the space to be
equally divided. Then, keeping the "0"
mark at the left margin of your space, slant
the ruler downward on the right margin until
the inch markers equal the number of spaces
you want for columns. Place a mark at each
inch along the slanted ruler, then lift the
ruler and draw vertical lines through those
markings.

Still another way to divide spaces and
draw parallel lines is with a "<u>lettering in-
strument</u>" offered by Dot Pasteup Supply. The
plastic template allows for drawing guide
lines from 1/16" to 2" in height.

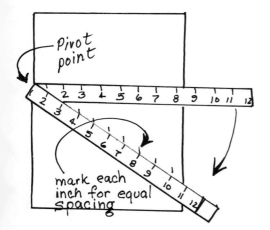

pivot
point

mark each
inch for equal
spacing

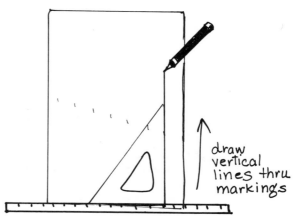

draw
vertical
lines thru
markings

PERMANENT LAYOUT BOARDS

Once you have your layout designed and artwork and headings collected, you may wish to make a permanent layout sheet or pasteup board. A permanent pasteup board is usually made on a heavier paper, similar to a 3"x5" recipe card in weight, on which your heading, address, phone, etc., remain constant.

After each printing, the copy and artwork are removed from the board and it is ready to use again.

I often make a few blank copies of my permanent layout board, and type my newsletter right on that copy for the next printing. The reproduction will not be as sharp as from the original, but it does work!

Graphic Products Corporation makes a number of "Border Boards" for use as permanent layout boards. There are many exciting borders to choose from, and the board is gridded with non-repro blue for easy pasteup.

A few of the BORDER BOARDS offered by
GRAPHIC PRODUCTS CORPORATION

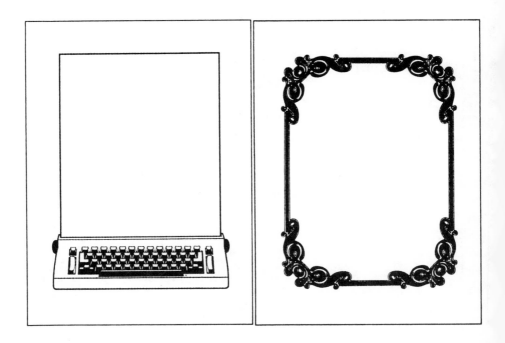

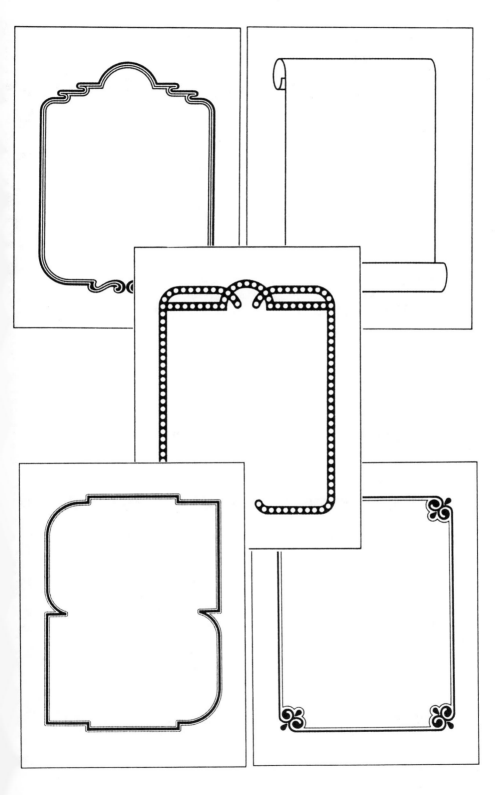

SUMMARY

1. Use black and white photos only for reproduction. Show your product in use; crop photos to what pertains to the subject at hand.

2. Cover photos with 85-line white copy screen prior to copying.

3. Line drawings can be reduced prior to pasteup, then shaded with shading film or by hand.

4. Clip art can be purchased, borrowed from newspapers and magazines, and found in libraries. No copyright infringements, please.

5. For large solid areas use masking film. White "transfer letters" can be applied to masking film for "drop out" effect.

6. Use a non-repro pen or pencil for markings that you do not want to show when photocopied.

7. Use bar charts or circle charts rather than line graphs for quantity comparisons.

8. Borders and arrows add interest and direct the reader's eye.

9. Use only clean, very black lettering/typing.

10. No smudges! Ink, glue, fingerprints, coffee stains—all will reproduce and make an unattractive mailer.

6 Layout & design

Now that you have selected a format, planned the promotion, written the copy and collected some artwork, you must decide what size paper to use and just where to put everything. That process is called "layout," or "design."

Choose a <u>paper size</u> that will be available and affordable to you now and in the future. Your basic choices will be from these three:

1. Standard typewriter-size paper, 8½"x 11". It is the most readily available, the most economical to use, and comes in a wide range of colors. Color costs more to have made than white, about one cent each page at the photo copy center. Standard typewriter size is easily folded into thirds, like a business letter, or folded in half. It can be stuffed into an envelope and mailed, or addressed on a blank side and mailed.

2. Legal size paper, 8½"x14". Legal size is also available at copy centers; sometimes

in white only. To get legal size in colored paper, you may have to seek it out at a stationery or office supply store or discount paper outlet. It will be more efficient for you to use paper that the copy center purchases in bulk and that they are likely to have available at all times.

Legal size paper can be folded in thirds, or fourths, for mailing.

3. Your third choice is 11"x17". This is a good size for printing brochures or pamphlets. Availability and color range will be limited at the copy center, and not all photo copy machines can handle the size. A quick phone call to your copy center will tell you. 11"x17" can be folded in half to measure 8½"x11", then folded into thirds or in half for addressing and mailing.

It's a good option to take if you're thinking about printing two 8½"x11" on both sides and stapling them together. Each side of an 11"x17" will hold two 8½"x11" pages, and no staples will be needed.

MAKING A DUMMY

A "dummy" is a rough draft of your mailer. Make it on paper the same size as your finished product with pencil sketches showing the placement of photos, illustrations, text or copy, and headings, etc. This placement is called a "layout."

Lightly fold your sample paper to the same size as your finished mailer is to be when ready for addressing and mailing. Next, hold the folded dummy before you, and visualize receiving it in the mail. Will you stuff it into envelopes or will you leave a side blank for addressing?

If you will be using envelopes, you are free to cover the entire paper, both sides if you like, with information. If you choose it to be a self-mailer, with the address placed on a blank side, then pencil in your return name and address in an upper left corner, and sketch in a rectangle where the mailing address will go. You can also draw a small square where the postage stamp will be.

Now open the mailer as you would if you had just received it. This is how your customer will open it, and right away he must see your most important message—your benefit to him. So you "design" the layout to accomplish just that!

Any composition, be it a fine arts painting or simple mail out flier, is done with purpose. It has a flow of line and design. It is calculated. It works. One of the easiest theories of design is what I call the "triangle theory."

A triangle is one of the oldest and most effective shapes used in design. Ancient Egyptians utilized it for the pyramids. Cooks in the old West used it to bring in the boys for dinner! You're going to use it to bring customers to your product or service, to draw the reader's eye through your mailer; from benefit, to motive, to name & location.

Triangles come in different shapes, but they all have only three sides! In the illustrations that follow, you'll notice that the triangle itself is not overtly apparent; it subtly lies behind the main composition or copy and artwork. Three seems to be a magic number for use in composition.

Try to place no more than three pieces of artwork on any one page, and face that artwork into the body of the page rather than toward the edges. Artwork can be a photo of a person or product, or a few lines of large type such as a heading. It can be a drawing or illustration of either a single large item or of a group or cluster of several small ones.

One cluster could simply be your business logo or illustration showing your name, location, phone, and hours.

Practice penciling a few triangle shapes onto some dummy pages. Then pencil in your heading (use large letters) somewhere in the top third of the page. You will have one or two spaces left next to the triangle corners where you can sketch in approximate sizes and shapes of your artwork.

It can be fun and beneficial for you to cut out your heading and artwork and spend some time repositioning each around different shaped triangles on your page. Move them around until something looks right to you. Cut your heading into two or three lines, if you have to, to make it fit the space.

There is no rule that says that headlines have to be a straight line, or that coupons have to be rectangular in shape. Would it help to reduce your artwork? Would it help to string-out your logo, address, phone and hours? Cut apart the heading, word by word, and reposition it several different ways. Then choose the one you like best.

Somewhere in the top third of your page, pencil-in the customer benefit. State it as simply as possible, in LARGE LETTERS.

Large letters will reinforce the reader's eye movement to start reading at that point. Clip art or photographs will also draw the eye, so it makes sense to place the large letters or heading next to your most important (dominant) artwork. Because we read from left to right, keep the heading on the left, and the artwork on the right. Not for the entire page, but at least for the top third of the layout.

A good place to get ideas is from newspapers and magazines. Look through them. Notice which ads catch your eye. Why? Was it a photo of somebody you thought for an instant you might know? People like to look at and read about people—that's why the supermarket "celebrity" papers are so popular.

Another trick is to close your eyes while turning the newspaper page. When the page is turned and in position, open your eyes and notice the first thing you see. Is it a bold headline? A photograph? An illustration? What was it that caught your eye?

How many phrases in advertisements you read ask questions? Do you feel compelled to respond? Most of us do, but most of us can't without becoming more informed, and of course the rest of the copy provides the information. First you're "hooked," and then you're informed.

Use the same tactics in your layout. Use what works.

Practice drawing triangle

layouts on your worksheet.

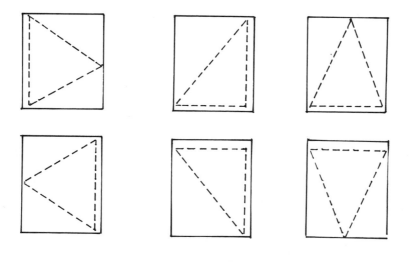

SAMPLE LAYOUT, 11x17

Facing in   *Facing out*

COUPON LAYOUT

There is no reason your coupon, if you choose to use one, could not be a small triangle at the bottom right corner of your page. It would in fact be much faster for the customer to cut off!

Your coupon can be round, like a hot-air balloon or a golf-ball. It could be written within the lines of a flower or tree, or shaped like a toy bear or a Valentine heart. Let your imagination take over, have some fun with your designing and layout, but remember that straight lines are faster to cut. It might be wise, then, to put your novel coupon-idea INSIDE a square or rectangle shape.

Whatever you decide, keep your coupon consistant. Not specifically in its shape, but in the same location on your layout.

Customers will come to look for it there. Pencil it onto your dummy for now, you can always change your mind later.

Have fun designing your coupons!

LOGO LAYOUT

Where is the best place to put your name and location? Put it either at the top or at the bottom of your mailer. Both places work fine, but it should be smaller type than your main customer benefit (headline) because it is of secondary importance. That may not be so to you, but to your reader the most important information is the benefit.

Once you hook the reader with your benefit and motivate him to come after it, then and only then does your name and location become important to him. He will seek it out; but that doesn't mean you should hide it! Logo type should be smaller than the main headline, but make it large enough to be easily read.

If your mailer is to be printed on both sides, then repeat your name and location again on the bottom of the second side. If you are doing a monthly newsletter, or quarterly, then your newsletter name should be at the top of page one.

The name of your newsletter should indicate what product or service it covers, but if you prefer to use a catchy one-word title or a piece of letterhead, then add a subtitle directly beneath it explaining what your newsletter is all about.

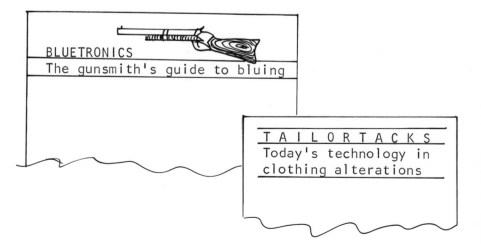

BLUETRONICS
The gunsmith's guide to bluing

TAILORTACKS
Today's technology in clothing alterations

If you are doing newsletters as a business, that is, selling subscriptions for news of a particular business or group, one good book to read is *Publishing News-letters* by Howard Penn Hudson (Charles Scribner's Sons, New York).

BUILDING FAMILIARITY

You'll recall that building familiarity with your customers is part of a promotional mailer's function. One way to do that is by printing a photo of your store or yourself in your mailer. Place it next to your store name and location, and put a caption beneath the photo, such as "Wally's Cakes" or "Wally Bygolly, Owner." (See Chapter Seven for handling photos and permanent layout boards).

ADDING OTHER INFORMATION

Other information, from the "bridge" to the "body" to a "bio" to the "close," will be in smaller print than your headline. All you need to do at this point is pencil in the basic shape or space available for that information to fit into, and a few notes to help you write your copy. Other information can be anecdotes about yourself or your business: things that would build a familiarity with your customer.

ONE COLUMN OR TWO?

A mailer printed on standard 8½"x11" paper can be designed with a single column of copy about six or seven inches in length (wide). Dividing that same page into two columns makes copy about three inches in length.

A comfortable length for average readers is 45 characters per line (about 3½").
Longer lines create eye fatigue and often
the reader looses interest. Your right
margin does NOT have to justified (even),
so making two columns on a 8½"x11" page is
rather easy to do.

Fold the paper lengthwise, or draw a
line down the center of the page with a
non-repro pen or pencil. Leave ample margins
on both sides of your columns; overcrowding
with copy or artwork can look cluttered
and amateurish. Mark your left and right
margins with a non-repro pen or pencil, and
type your copy between those lines only.

It does take a bit longer to type a
two column page, but your aim is to be professional without being "slick" in the mailings you send out. Professionalism empha-
sizes your sincerity in business—and if
you don't take your business seriously, no
one else will either.

*Newsletters can be one column
or two. Leave a half-inch space
between columns in a two-column
format.*

PLACEMENT OF ARTWORK

Photos and illustrations can be used in your mailer to fill in around your basic triangle shape, and should be varied in content. If you show one large product or photo in one space, make the next one a collection or grouping of several small items. You can also put seasonal artwork (a Santa for Christmas, a robin for Spring), in a space rather than product photos.

To have some fun with club newsletters, put in a few photos of the last gathering! You'll be surprised at the reception your "new" newsletter receives, and what's more, people will save them to show to friends. And that could lead to increased membership!

BORDERS

If your dummy could use some "packaging" or pulling together to please the eye, try adding a border. Pencil one in, whether it goes completely around your material, only on the top and bottom, or maybe just on two sides at right angles to each other.

Here again, flip through some news-paper ads to see how the use of borders and dressing has helped them stand out. Graphic Products Corporation offers a large selection of border designs that can be burnished onto your final pasteup. (See also the section on Permanent Layout Boards in Chapter Five).

APPLYING DRAWING TAPES AND BORDERS
(Courtesy of Letraset®)

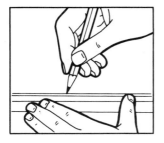

If required, a guide line can be drawn or the tape pen can be moved along the edge of a ruler. Position the tape end firmly to the art surface and holding the dispenser, draw along the guide line or ruler.

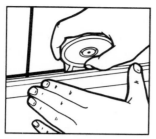

A steady pull should be used. (Do not draw too taut, as there is a risk of thinner tapes snapping.) A constant firm pressure on the dispenser will adhere the tape to the art surface.

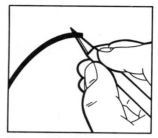

Tapes can be re-positioned before burnishing. Once burnished, they will remain in position.

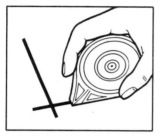

When producing corners, a flat, tight join can be created by overlapping the ends of each line.

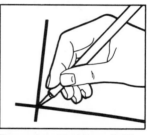

Then make a 45 degree cut at the corner—from the outside corner to the inside one. Remove the two excess ends and let the tape ends fall into place. You'll find they match exactly.

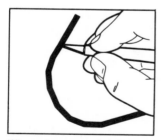

When using a normally inflexible tape for curves, you can use a knife to cut out the bulges made by the tape. This method is less helpful the wider the tape and the tighter the curve.

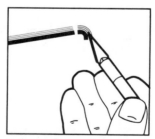

Until recently, curved or more elaborate corners had to be created by hand or ignored. Now you can use Letraline Border tapes in a variety of styles and use the matching Corner tape to achieve a perfect fit.

PAGE NUMBERS

If your mailer is two or more separate pages of information, number the pages beginning with page two. It's true that people are easily confused, and numbering the pages will help them follow your intent. If you have copy printed on the reverse side of page one, label it "Page 2." The next page of course will be "Page 3" and so on.

PUNCHING HOLES

Very often readers can be encouraged to save each newsletter you send simply by seeing a set of holes prepunched for a three ring binder.

You do not need to offer them the binder, but you will have to allow room for the holes when making your layout.

Economical three-hole punches can be purchased at local stationery supply stores.

TYPESETTING

Typesetting, whether typewritten, hand lettered, or made with transfer lettering, is that clean black copy on crisp white paper that will be cut and pasted to your layout sheet.

Using your dummy layout as a guide, mark a fine line around the areas allowed for copy with a non-repro pen or pencil. Type or hand letter within those fine blue lines, keeping the ink black and the copy clean. When your typing or lettering is dry, it can then be cut and pasted to your final pasteup board.

Keep in mind when "typesetting" that using both upper and lower case letters makes for faster reading. It does not matter if your right margin is justified (all lines ending at the same point, forming the right margin) or not. Ragged right margins make for easier reading.

If you are using a typewriter that has only very large type and you think that it is too large, type the copy out and have it reduced at the copy center before pasting it.

Hand printing or lettering is not uncommon in business practices. Many small or elite restaurants hand letter their menus. Calligraphy can be effective, but it becomes monotonous when overused, so keep it to headings or special flyers. Your main goal is readability at the customer level.

For headlines, you can use calligraphy or transfer lettering. I often burnish the dry transfer onto a piece of tracing paper (you'll want to draw a base line on the tracing paper with a non-repro pen), cut, and paste on my layout. (See also Chapter Five).

In addition to headlines (headings) you have saved from magazines or fashioned from transfer lettering, headlines can be made on a lettering machine. The machines cost from $300 to $600 or more, but you can buy a strip with your choice of words on it at many office supply stores. The machine has a large round dial on the front, with which you select the letters. They are then printed on a transparent strip of film, which is adhered to your layout sheet.

READY TO PASTE?

When your layout is done, when you're satisfied with the placement of headline, artwork, and copy, then you are ready to pasteup your mechanical.

The mechanical consists of black headlines, artwork, and type pasted on a layout board or white paper (pasteup sheet) and is camera-ready. That means no errors, no smudges.

You can take it to the copy center or print shop with no apologies. However, this time when you're waiting in line, you will begin to notice mechanicals presented that DO need some apologizing!

CAN YOU MAKE IT BETTER?

Here's a little test to see what you've learned so far. The illustrations are composites of mechanicals that I have encountered while waiting in line at my favorite full service copy center. Can you change them for the better?

This one was presented by Mrs. Churchworker. She ordered 100 copies and rushed out to post them around town in an effort to draw newcomers to her church picnic.

St. Bob's Church

Picnic on Sunday, June 23rd. Public is welcome. 3pm at Mary's Park. Bring hot dish and table service. Free Coffee! Offering $2.00 each.

Here's how Mrs. Churchworker might have attracted more folks to the picnic.

The benefit (picnic) should be the most visible headline, rather than the name of the church. Remember, your name is most important to you, but secondary to the reader. I would not go out of my way to read about a church I don't know. I have my own. Now, if it was MY church's name on that flyer, I would have checked it out; but then again, being a member, I would probably already know about the picnic!

Was Mrs. Churchworker's flyer <u>targeted</u> to the right audience? Here's a quick alternative. Same time spent designing, writing, and pasting. But with different effect:

Here's another example. This flyer was for a ladies' apparel store, and she made the same mistake! Can you correct it?

Original   Revised

SUMMARY

1. Know what size paper you want to use and get a sample.

2. Fold paper into a dummy and begin layout design. Position and reposition cut out facsimiles of artwork, headlines, and copy.

3. Prepare artwork and type. Customer benefit is done in largest type. Business name and location can be next largest, if desired. If you are giving two benefits, use large letters again for the second benefit.

4. Write the copy. Keep it simple. Too much information can overwhelm the reader. To limit your flyer to one benefit or subject is best. Newsletters, however, may cover several pieces of information or benefits.

5. Sell the benefit. The customer will then find you.

7 Pasteup & supplies

In order to do your pasteup or "mech-anical," you'll need some supplies. Much of what you need can be found in artists' supply stores and college book stores.

The supplies are called "graphic arts supplies," and you may be lucky enough to locate a store that deals only in them!

I buy most of my supplies through the mail. It saves travel time, parking fees, and gasoline. And it's nice to have the supplies delivered right to my door!

Sources I have used are Dot Pasteup Supply, The Printers Shopper, and Dick Blick, to name a few. You will find their addresses in the Appendix and can write to them for a catalog.

The minimum supplies you'll need to start a pasteup are <u>crisp white paper</u>, which can be used for typing or hand lettering your copy onto, and also as a layout sheet. The other thing you'll need is <u>rubber cement</u>. Anything other than rubber cement or wax for pasteup will wrinkle your copy and cause black lines and smudges to appear when printed.

Rubber cement comes in a jar with a brush attached to the lid, and in quarts and gallons, and in a convenient little tube called "Glutube." It allows you to remove and reposition your artwork and copy for a long time after it has been applied.

Commercial printers use hot wax, which also allows the repositioning of copy. There are hand waxers available as well as handy glu-sticks or wax-sticks that can be used cold.

You must have pens and pencils for artwork and borders. Get ones with permanent, dense black ink or use dip pens with India ink. Use a metal ruler for cutting against; several kinds are available. There are plastic see-through rulers, like a centering ruler, that are handy but should never be used for a cutting guide.

A paper cutting scissors is handy for chop-jobs. An X-acto knife or Proedge knife works better for cutting around copy and artwork prior to fitting and pasting. Proedge, X-acto, and Grifhold all make swivel knives that are wonderful for cutting curved artwork.

Cellophane tape used for joining parts of your copy that have been cut apart to rearrange; especially when making your paper dummy. Other tapes that will be useful are white paper tapes, for covering unwanted marks or edges on your pasteup, and drafting tape for holding your layout sheet in place. Drafting tape looks like masking tape, but has less tack and can be removed with no damage to the underlying paper.

Correcting fluids or "white out" will prove very handy indeed! Get the kind made for photo copies—it is water based, and can be thinned with water. Use it for masking unwanted smudges or marks on your pasteup. It can also be used to correct typing errors, although lift-off correction (where the carbon ink is actually removed from the paper) is better. Many typewriters now have this feature.

Some of the knives offered by PROEDGE

PO No.1 LIGHT DUTY KNIFE
4 7/8", aluminum handle with P11 blade.

PO No.2 MEDIUM DUTY KNIFE
5" Aluminum handle with P24 blade.

PO No.3 PEN KNIFE
All aluminum with clear plastic cap,
pocket clip and P10 blade.

PO No.5 HEAVY DUTY KNIFE
4 1/4" long, aluminum lock, plastic handle
with P19 blade & blade storage in handle.

PO No.6 HEAVY DUTY KNIFE
4 3/4" long all aluminum handle,
with P19 blade.

PO No.7 WOODCARVING KNIFE
4 3/4" long, aluminum lock, contoured
plastic handle, with P101 blade.

"FREE FLOW" SWIVEL KNIFE
5" aluminum handle, blade rotates
freely 360º.

UTILITY KNIFE
Retractable, reversible, replaceable blade.
Molded pocket clip on handle.

EXECUTIVE No.1
5" long anodized aluminum handle,
improved blade release system,
with P11 blade.

PO No.1 SG KNIFE
PO No.1 light duty knife with clear plastic
non-roll safety guard.

PO No.2 SG KNIFE
PO No.2 medium duty knife with clear
plastic non-roll safety guard.

FLOWER MATE KNIFE
5" aluminum handle with non-roll safety
neck and P26 blade.

PATTERN KNIFE
For stained glass. Holds 2-P19 blades at a
.032" point spread (.093 chuck available).

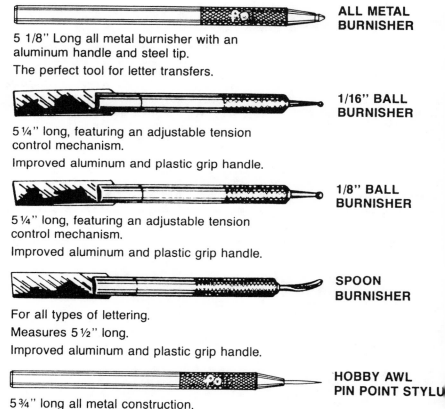

ALL METAL BURNISHER

5 1/8" Long all metal burnisher with an aluminum handle and steel tip.

The perfect tool for letter transfers.

1/16" BALL BURNISHER

5¼" long, featuring an adjustable tension control mechanism.

Improved aluminum and plastic grip handle.

1/8" BALL BURNISHER

5¼" long, featuring an adjustable tension control mechanism.

Improved aluminum and plastic grip handle.

SPOON BURNISHER

For all types of lettering.

Measures 5½" long.

Improved aluminum and plastic grip handle.

HOBBY AWL PIN POINT STYLU

5¾" long all metal construction.

Heat treated point for long, durable life.

Below is a sampling of the many graphic supplies offered by The Printers Shopper

Glue Stick

Rubber Cement in a Tube

CORRECTION FLUID

THE BEST LITTLE ORGANIZER WE'VE SEEN

All your graphic arts tools can be right at your finger tips with the little GIANT ORGANIZER.

ROTO TRAY

Holds every item you can reach for in a day's work within it's 10" circle.

BLUE MIRAGE NON REPRO MARKER

NEW

BEROL NON-REPRODUCING BLUE PEN

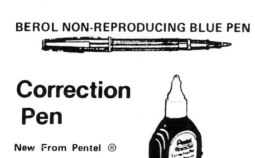

Correction Pen

New From Pentel ®

WEIGHTED DISPENSERS

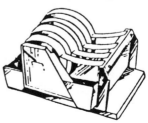

Prior to pasteup, check any typewriter corrections that have been made with correcting fluid. If you can see the original type, or error, in normal daylight, so will the camera and copy machine. I have salvaged such corrections by retyping the correct word onto a self-stick white label, cutting carefully around it, and placing it over the original type.

Masking films are red films used to cover large areas that are to be printed solid black. The film is lightly pressed onto the layout, trimmed to size and excess removed, then burnished in place. Results from masking films tend to be better when used in offset printing, but photo copier gets acceptable results.

A copy screen will be needed if you are going to use photos. It is a clear film that has been printed with white dots and comes in 65, 85, or 100-line (number of dots per linear inch). White shading film is like a copy screen but printed on a self-adhesive film. It comes in terms of dots per inch (get 85-line) and also in percentages from 10% to 90%, with 90% being the most dense. Get 30%.

A copy screen or white shading film is placed over black and white photos prior to reproducing on a photo copier. A printer will want to use a half-tone, and can make it for you.

For shadows and backgrounds on artwork, you can use black shading films. They are like white shading films but with black dots printed 27.5 to 85 per inch. (27.5 line to 85 line). Densities run from 10% to 70% with 70% being the most dense. For normal use, choose 20% or 30%. Shading films are self adhesive, and can be cut to size around your artwork, excess removed, then burnished.

Non-repro pens and pencils write in light blue that will not reproduce on the copy machine or with the printer's camera.

Burnishers are tools used to rub transfer lettering or clip art from the backing sheets.

Layout sheets (also called pasteup sheets) are white sheets gridded with non-repro blue lines. Your final pasteup will be

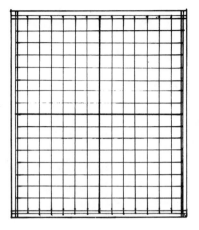

Layout sheets or boards are white with non-repro blue grids. You can purchase them or make your own.

put onto a layout sheet. You can make your own on white paper or illustration board lined with a non-repro blue pen. (See Chapter Five on how to draw lines). Layout boards are the same as layout sheets but on heavier stock. They are good to use when your heading or other pasteup material remains constant from printing to printing. Simply remove the copy that changes and replace it with the new.

A light box or light table is a light source behind a frosted glass or plastic window over which you may align copy and artwork with grids on layout sheets. For details on buying or making your own light box, see Chapter Five.

Tracing paper is translucent paper used to trace designs, etc., without the need for a light box. It's also good to use over your pasteup for a final rub down.

A few other things you can put to use are a tweezers for picking up and placing small pieces of copy or artwork, an engineer's triangle, one with a right angle (90°), and Artgum eraser for changes in your dummy layout, and a rubber cement pickup for removing excess rubber cement. You can also remove

it by rubbing with your clean finger, or
saving all the rubber cement crumbs and fash-
ioning them into a little ball.

You won't need everything right at
first, but once you get started and order a
few catalogs, it's amazing how your appetite
for graphic supplies increases!

PREPARATION FOR PASTEUP

You'll want to be organized before beginning your pasteup. It's NOT going to be
as critical as stirring chocolate fudge, however. You will have time to reconsider and
reposition pieces of artwork or copy. But
it helps to have all the parts of your project
ready before you open that jar of rubber cement
(which, by the way, should be closed after
each little use).

Gather up all the components: your
dummy layout, your white layout sheet, artwork, copy, scissors or metal ruler and art
knife, photos, copy screen, and any other
items you think you might need. Have a rag
handy to wipe the excess rubber cement from
your fingers.

Artwork and copy should be trimmed
neatly prior to pasteup, leaving a margin
of about 1/8 inch.

Make a final inspection of your artwork and copy. Any small marks or smudges
can be covered after pasteup. Anything
worse than that should possibly be redone
before you paste. Both carbon film ribbon
and inked artwork will smear when pasting
if it hasn't been allowed to dry for a few
hours.

There's only one more thing to do before
opening that jar of rubber cement. Prepare
your layout sheet.

PASTING THE MECHANICAL

The first thing you must do on your
layout sheet is provide "grab" room for

the copy machine or printer. Either will
need at least a 1/4" margin on all sides of
your mechanical. Use a non-repro pen and
a ruler to draw a 1/4" margin on all four
sides of your paper. Your copy and artwork
will be pasted within those lines.

*The first step in the
pasteup is marking a
¼" margin on all four
sides of the layout
sheet. Use nonrepro
blue.*

Next, again using your non-repro pen,
sketch in the layout you made on the dummy.
When you become more at ease with doing
pasteups, you can skip this step and move
on to the next.
Now you can open that rubber cement!
Starting with the largest piece of artwork
or copy, put a small dot or two of rubber
cement on the back and gently put each on
your layout sheet in its prescribed place.
Then check each piece for fit; if there are
any overlapping edges, now is the time to
trim them back. Overlapping edges will
produce little black lines when printed.
When your copy and artwork is all
fitted to size (you can fit the very small
pieces during pasteup), remove them one at
a time and apply a stroke of rubber cement
around the edges on the back side, leaving
a 1/16" margin. A good rule of thumb is
to start with the largest piece and work
your way down to the smallest piece.
Replace the cemented piece and position

squarely in its place, aligning with grid
lines. Hold a clean sheet of paper over
the layout and gently smooth down each
piece with your hand as you go. You'll do
it again after all the pieces have been
applied to the page, but a bit firmer,
using a nylon or plastic brayer. Or the
spine of a paperback book. Or the side of
a smooth pen.

For a permanent heading, such as you
would use for a monthly newsletter or bulletin, use a layout board. This is heavier
than a layout sheet, and you can remove
everything but the heading after your piece
has been printed each time.

Layout boards can be used several times
and save you the time of pasting up your
heading each month.

When your pasteup is complete, and any
masking films or shading films have been
added and borders applied, do your final
rub down. Cover your layout with a clean
piece of paper (tracing paper works well)
and smooth with a bone folding knife or the
side of a pencil. You need not press extremely hard, but firm enough to make sure everything, especially all edges, is well adhered. Loose edges can cause little black
lines to appear on the printed copy.

While your pasteup is drying, study it
for any spots or smudges that need to be
covered with correction fluid. A misplaced
line can be covered with white paper tape.

Remove any excess rubber cement with
your finger or a rubber cement pickup.
You'll want a clean black and white copy
for printing.

Stand back and admire your work for a
moment, you deserve it! Then slip it into
a file folder or large envelope, and you're
off to the copy shop or printer!

SUMMARY

1. Gather all the supplies you'll need for
   your pasteup.

2. Gather and trim all the components of artwork, photos, and copy, leaving a 1/8" margin.

3. Tape your layout sheet down. Draw a 1/4" margin on all four sides before starting pasteup.

4. Place and fit artwork and copy, trimming away any overlapping edges before final pasteup. Follow the layout on your dummy.

5. Make a final rub down when all artwork and copy is applied by covering with a clean sheet of paper and smoothing firmly with hand, bone folding knife, or the side of a pencil. The spine of a paperback book will work, too.

6. Final check before printing: is all the information there and correct? Is the copy and artwork square with the layout grid? Are all corrections and smudges covered with white? Excess glue removed? Are all edges down good? No overlapping edges? Now is the time to correct!

7. Off to the print shop: cover with a clean sheet, slip into a file folder or large envelope to prevent marking and folding.

8 Printing, folding & fastening

Your mechanical is finished and you're ready to have it printed. You have several choices for printing—which you may want to consider prior to doing your pasteup.

Your options include: The Ditto machine, the Mimeograph, the photo copy machine, or the printer, who will probably use an offset press.

If you are producing a newsletter or bulletin for your club and club policy dictates that you use their Ditto machine, then that is what you do.

<u>Ditto machines</u> are not as commonplace as they were in my early school days. Oh how I loved to help the teacher by turning the crank on that little machine and watch the purple-inked copies magically appear! But don't think they've disappeared altogether. I still get a newsletter every month that has been lovingly turned out by a Ditto machine.

It's been said that the Ditto makes

copies of lesser quality than printing and therefore may infer that your product or service is also of lesser quality. It's true they can't match the work of today's photo copiers, but go ahead and use it for your club bulletins. Think twice before using it to promote your business.

The Mimeograph is also retiring into the past, but like the Ditto, you may be required to use it. Here again, you must "cut" a stencil for the Mimeograph either with your typewriter or stylus, place it on the drum, pour in the ink, set up the reams of paper, and crank away. If you're lucky, your club has an electric crank. These early printing appliances can be messy and time consuming, but work well for clubs and churches where costs must be kept to a minimum and the labor is volunteered.

The average small business person will want to use photo copy process or a printer.

Photo copy centers will be full-service or self-service. They will offer you a wide variety of papers, both in size and in color. Prices start with 8½"x11" white paper, and increase depending on color, size, and texture. Card stock is also available in white and colors, and can be used for inexpensive business cards, pamphlets, or catalog covers.

The copy center will print only in black. A word of caution is in order here— the toner (ink) can rub off onto your hands and clothing. Hands can be washed, but it's difficult to remove the black smudges from clothing without making them worse! Advise the dry cleaners accordingly if should happen to you!

You may want to call or visit a few copy centers for prices before having your mailer printed. Because you'll find them competitive in pricing, the one closest to you may be the best choice. Take your mechanical, along with rubber cement, white correcting fluid, a scissors, and cellophane tape. Ask to see a "proof" or single copy before

giving the go-ahead on printing. A proof
will let you see any corrections or cover-
ups that need to be made before printing,
and allows the assistant to adjust the
copy machine for optimum results.

If the copy center has more than one
brand of copier, and the proof you see does
not meet your expectations, ask to see a
proof from another machine. Some will give
better copies than others, especially if
reproducing photographs.

After you have touched up your original for smudges or lines, proceed with the
printing.

Copy centers often like to keep printing
orders to a minimum of 500, and they may
ask you to come back later to pick it up.
At this writing, the average cost of a white
8½"x11" copy in the Seattle area is 5¢ each.
Pastel colors sell for 6¢ each, bright colors

Today's modern photocopy machines
can print on several paper sizes

and legal size for more. Card stock runs
10¢ per sheet. Double the price if you're
printing on both sides.

A self-service copy center will also
offer a selection of papers and colors,
but you will do the work. Ask the assistant
for help in learning to run the machine and
even in adjusting the lightness for best
results. I have found the self-service copy
centers to be no less expensive than full-
service ones, and in some cases are actually
higher priced.

When you reach the magic number of

ordering 500 copies, it would be wise to contact a printer for a bid.

A _printer_ can typeset your copy or print from your camera ready mechanical. (Typesetting is expensive). It will take longer than the copy center, but if you plan your promotion schedule and pasteup well ahead of time, your mailer should be printed and ready to mail in plenty of time.

Not all printers will want to print small jobs, and will do so only because they hope to get your future, bigger business. Their lack of interest or dedication may show up in lack of quality in your printing job. But this is not to say that there are not some very concientious printers in the marketplace.

While prices at the copy centers are competitive and rather standard, prices at a print shop can vary a great deal. You will want to telephone three or four to get bids.

Volume sells in printing—the more copies you have printed the less expensive per copy they will be. Presses are designed for specific jobs, so you will want to locate a printer whose press is designed to do what you want.

You'll also want to locate one who keeps the size and color of paper you want in stock (buys it in bulk) and the color of printing ink. Special orders for small quantities of paper and ink will cost you more. So will folding.

Many printers have folding machines, which will save you time and sore fingers for a minimal extra charge. If you have lots of extra time to fold, you can do it yourself. From personal experience, I can tell you that hand folding anything over 500 copies is a backbreaking job! Even using a bone folding knife doesn't get as sharp a crease as the printer's folding machine. It makes a tight, smooth fold that can be mailed without staples or tape.

And what about staples and tape? Mailers that are staped in one corner are cumbersome to fold, stack, mail, and the U.S.Postal Service doesn't like them (the staples).

A two or three page mailer folded in thirds by machine will travel through the mail without much trouble. If you must fasten your mailer closed, use a short piece of cellophane tape or a self-adhesive sticker folded over the bottom edge. Once your customer has opened it, he'll find the unstapled mailer easier to read than the stapled one; especially if it's printed on both sides of the pages. And you've saved the cost, time, and trouble of stapling.

Another factor in the printer's price is timing. If you can wait for five days or so, the printer can work your job into his schedule. If you want a rush job, however, it will cost you more money: the printer will have to work overtime, or hire extra help, or chance delaying another customer's job in order to print yours. This can be a real problem if he has only one press!

So how do you locate a printer? The first place to look is to fellow merchants or businesses. Ask them what printer they use and if they are pleased with the service. Family and friends may know of a printer (that's no guarantee the service is good), or you might want to phone a few publishers of newsletters and other mailers you have received and ask what printer they use. Then there's the Yellow Pages, under "Printers." Pick three or four.

Call and ask for bids. They will need to know (1) what size and color paper you want, (2) what color ink you want, (3) how many copies you want, (4) do they need to be collated (sorted and assembled) or folded, and (5) will there be any stapling or fastening? You can ask for an itemized bid, which will list the printer's services separately, then omit the ones you can do yourself to save money. Before you hang up, find out how soon they can start and complete your job, and what the minimum charge is for printing.

Printers who are interested in new accounts will be happy to send you not only the bid, but also a sample of the paper in the color you want, and a sample of similar work they have done. Don't expect to get a sample of the color paper you want with the color ink you want, but you can ask! When you get the sample, look it over for grayness in the printing job—is the printing faded? Is the ink uneven? Is it black (or dense color) throughout the printing job? Is the copy straight on the paper?

When your bids are in and you've examined the samples of work, choose the printer. Consider not just the least expensive in dollars, but the quality of their work, do they deliver (save you time and money) or is the print shop conveniently located to you? Can they do half-tones on photos if you should need it? And will they extend you credit?

Pay no more than 50% down when leaving your printing job, and ask for 30 days on the balance. If the balance is due on delivery, hold payment until you have inspected the work and accept it as is. Withholding payment of the balance may be your only leverage to have printing or typesetting errors corrected (which means reprinting). Errors that were submitted on your mechanical are "on you."

Printers have been known to forfeit payment of some or all of the balance due if they don't meet your deadline.

On the other hand, you need to develop a good working relationship with your printer, so when the work and service is good, pay up when due and be polite. You can learn a lot from him! Just remember that you're not married, and you are free to change printers if need be.

When your mailers are returned, including your original mechanical, you're ready to address and mail!

FOLDING

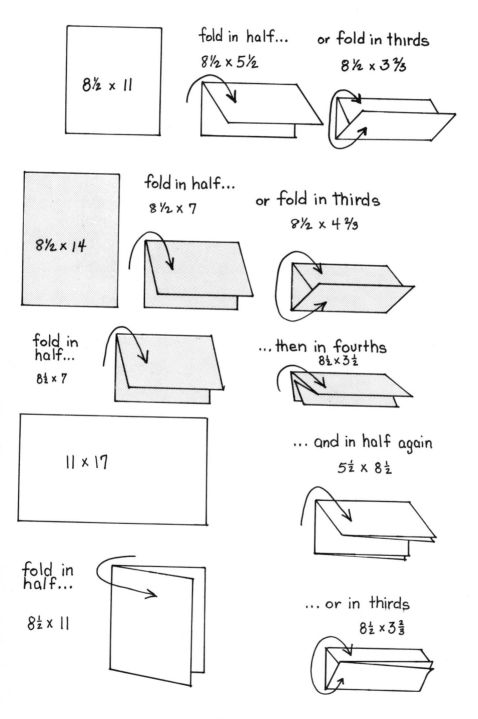

8½ x 11

fold in half...
8½ x 5½

or fold in thirds
8½ x 3⅔

8½ x 14

fold in half...
8½ x 7

or fold in thirds
8½ x 4⅔

fold in half...
8½ x 7

...then in fourths
8½ x 3½

11 x 17

... and in half again
5½ x 8½

fold in half...
8½ x 11

... or in thirds
8½ x 3⅔

SUMMARY

1. The copy center is fast and convenient. Take along rubber cement,
   correction fluid (white), scissors,
   and tape. Ask for a "proof," make
   any necessary corrections to your
   mechanical and print. Keep the ink
   away from your clothing. Consider a
   printer if making 500 copies or more.

2. The printer can use colored ink and can
   fold for mailing. He can also make
   halftones of photos. Call three
   printers for bids; get samples of their
   work; arrange deadlines and payment
   terms before leaving the order; get
   original mechanical back after printing.

---

*The PRINT GOCCO RISO PRINTER can be used to add
color to your mailer or to print the entire message.*

*This screen-type print machine is easy to use. Art-
work or copy is engraved on a screen
by exposure to brilliant flash,
ink is added, and printing can
begin.*

*For more information on the RISO
PRINT GOCCO PRINTER, write to
the Polycor Corporation.
(Address in Appendix)*

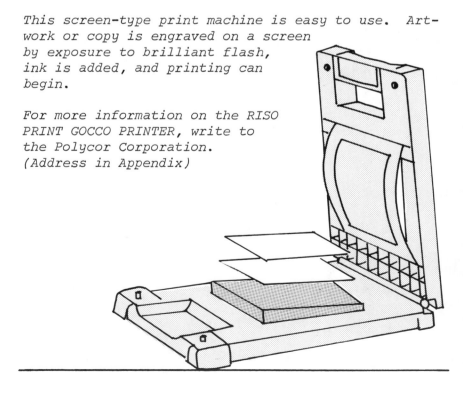

9 Mailing

Your material has been pasted, printed, folded, and is ready to be addressed and mailed. Again your head spins with questions—what's the best way to do it? Do I need to use bulk mail? How does it work? How much can I save?

This chapter will provide some answers and places to look for answers. We'll talk about mailing services, mailing lists, addressing your mailers, and of course the UNITED STATES POSTAL SERVICE—from first class to bulk rates.

MAILING SERVICES

A Mailing Service is a company that will mail your product for you. They often will fold, address, sort and carry to the Post Office. You can find Mailing Services in the Yellow Pages, and should call a few to get estimates on folding, stuffing, sealing, stamping, etc. It may be the answer if you are very short on time and/or help.

MAILING LISTS

The best mailing list is of course to your "target" audience. That means the ones that are most likely to buy your product or service. If you are just starting out in business, your beginning list will be to friends and relatives. It's also called your "Christmas card list." With those mailers you should ask for referrals, like "...if you know someone who might be interested in this, please pass it along to them." You may be surprized at the results it will bring, for each of your friends knows about 250 people of which one or two "might be interested."

Keep your "ear to the ground," as it were, for possible customers. Listen not only to relatives and friends, but also to your present customers, the people you do business with, the people you worship with, the people you play with, and even the people you do nothing with. The ones you don't know. When you recognize the mentioning of a potential customer, ask for the name and address for your mailing list.

You're simply asking for a referral, and you'll find that most of the time folks are eager to help you get started. Community newspapers and magazines will often mention a person compatible to your product or service. There are lists of marriages, births, deaths, notices of military accomplishment, employment promotions, new businesses, and businesses that are calling it quits. There is something for everyone if you learn how to recognize it.

If you want to mail to a particular section of town, or a neighborhood, you can find the names and addresses in a "reverse" directory at the library. Names are listed by street address or phone number, and indications are given for income brackets, home ownership, and employment status.

For some, the target audience will be found in municipal, county, or state records, like building permits, and vehicle registration. (Buy an RV and soon you'll be on all the RV resorts mailing lists!).

You can also rent or swap lists with

your neighboring merchants, if they agree. To avoid duplicates, separate mailings from your list and your neighbor's by a week or ten days. You can rent a list from a large mailing list company, targeted to a select group of names and addresses, often listed by profession. You pay per name, anywhere from 10¢ to $2.00 or more with a minimum number of names you must rent. There is the advantage that they come preaddressed on self-stick labels.

There will be "plants" in the lists—certain names and addresses that will report to the mailing list company if you use the list more times than you paid to do. And if you do, expect to get a bill for another rental! You can use names again of those who actually respond and buy from you.

For more information, write to one or more of the mailing list companies shown in the Appendix of this book.

It's always a good idea to start a mailing list when you start your business. Record names and addresses off of checks before you deposit them; ask cash or charge card purchasers if they would like to be on your mailing list; have an in-store promotion with a drawing for a free product or service, then save the names and addresses requested on the drawing slips and add them to your list; keep a sign-up sheet where it can be seen and voluntarily used. Sometimes the mailing lists you make yourself are the best ones. Keep them current, and transfer names to mailing label master sheets prior to each mailer you do. Sheets can be sorted by zip codes (handy when using bulk mail), alphabetically, or by active, inactive, and prospect. It is time consuming to keep a mailing list up to date without a computer, yet that's a pretty small reason to invest in one. Call a few "Secretarial Services" listed in the Yellow Pages and ask how much they charge to set up and maintain your mailing list on their computer. You'll have

to know how many names you have, but it may
be worth your while to submit updated information and let the secretarial service print
your mailing labels.

Your other choice is to do the addressing yourself!

ADDRESSING

Besides using a mailing service or
secretarial service, there are a couple of
ways you can address your mailers.

One is by hand. It is time consuming,
but it shows the recipient you gave a little
more of yourself to the material you're
sending. Always use ink—a ball point pen
does a good job, and it won't smear in the
rain like some nylon tip markers.

Anything that makes it easier for the
letter carrier to deliver your material should
be used.

AVERY makes mailing labels on an 8½"x11"
sheet, with 33 labels to a sheet. You can
handprint or typewrite an original listing,
or master sheet, which can then be repro-
duced at a copy center, on a fresh sheet
of labels, for about 35¢ per sheet. Ask
the copy center assistant for a master
sheet; one on which black lines are ruled
that correspond to the edges of the labels.
Simply type on a plain piece of paper put
over the master sheet, listing one name and
address in each square. This will be your
master list, and can be quickly copied onto
a sheet of labels at the copy center.

You can buy a packet of Avery labels
at your stationery or office supply store,
which includes a master sheet. This is great
if you have your own copy machine that will
handle labels; if not, and you don't use
labels very often, then either have the
labels printed ahead of time or let the
copy center do it for you on fresh ones.
Old labels tend to jam the machine.

Avery will send you more information on
their labels. See the Appendix for the mailing address.

I have addressed up to 500 mailers by hand only because I was waiting out a slack retail period and could give the time. A hand addressed mailer does seem to receive more attention, but I found that once my customers began to recognize my mailer (consistant format), the use of labels made no difference. They did not consider it "junk mail."

Labels can be used on envelopes as well as the self-mailer. As mentioned before, envelopes add a bit more expense, but you can remove and recirculate those mailers that happen to be returned to you. Just add new postage! You should know that not all postage rates allow for the return of un-deliverable mail.

POSTAGE

Whether first class or bulk rate, your mailer must conform to the standards of the United States Postal Service.

You can buy a roll of one hundred first class stamps, or consider using bulk mail when you have at least 200 identical pieces. Ask the Postal Service for Publication 113 *First-Class, Third-Class and Fourth-Class bulk mailings*.

"If you routinely mail large volumes," the publication says, "you should subscribe to the *Domestic Mail Manual* and to the *Postal Bulletin*. To order, write to the Superintendent of Documents, Government Printing Office, Washington, D.C. 20402-0001. Ask for subscription information.

The regulations for bulk mail are many. Because they are so thoroughly explained in Publication 113, I shall not attempt to detail them here. Suffice it to say it is wise to (1) read through the publication before you design your mailer; (2) know that you must have a minimum of 200 pieces and that they must be identical; (3) know you will do all the sorting and marking and delivery to the Post Office, and (4) know you will have to pay a yearly fee for a bulk mail permit.

Not all Post Offices accept bulk mail, so call the local branch to find out which one in your area does accept it. Then you might like to talk to the Bulk Mail Acceptance Clerk at that branch for further help.

How do you know when to use bulk mail? Use it when the savings outweigh any connotations of junk mail. You'll need to do some arithmetic to figure the economy of bulk mail; it depends on how many pieces you mail, to what zip codes you mail, and the frequency of those mailings—it is impossible to figure it to the cent!

There is also a yearly permit fee, which is good for the calendar year only. That means that whether you purchase your permit in January or October, it will expire on December 31st.

The only sensible way to calculate savings is by estimate, and on a yearly basis. You'll need to consider (1) number of pieces to be mailed, (2) the average cost of postage per piece, and (3) how many mailings can be done under a current permit. Your formula would look like this:

Total yearly postage, FIRST CLASS =
number of pieces to be mailed X first class
postage each X number of mailings per year

Total yearly postage, BULK RATE =
number of pieces to be mailed X average
bulk postage each X number of mailings
per year + yearly permit fee

For example: in 1982 I owned a retail shop, and sent a one to two page newsletter monthly. First Class postage at that time was 22¢ each piece. My newsletters went for Third Class bulk mail, at an average of 11¢ each. The yearly permit fee was $50. Suppose I began mailing in December, with 200 pieces. This is how the formula would work:

FIRST CLASS POSTAGE:	
Number of pieces to be mailed:	200
Postage, each piece:	X .22
Number of mailings per year:	X 1
TOTAL FIRST CLASS POSTAGE:	= 44.00

BULK MAIL POSTAGE:	
Number of pieces to be mailed:	200
Average postage each piece:	X .11
Number of mailings per year:	X 1
Yearly permit fee:	+ 50.00
TOTAL BULK RATE POSTAGE:	= 72.00

You can see the bulk rate is actually higher, because it doesn't pay to buy a permit for only one month's use. Or does it? Suppose my mailing list numbered 2000.

	FIRST CLASS	BULK RATE
Number of pieces	2000	2000
Postage each	X .22	X .11
	$ 440.00	$ 220.00
Bulk permit fee	.00	50.00
TOTAL POSTAGE per year	$ 440.00	$ 270.00

Because the number of pieces is much more, the savings amounts to $170.00 even on a single mailing.

When you purchase your bulk mail permit, you will be given a form on which to figure the exact amount of postage due. You will pay that before depositing your tray of sorted mail with the Bulk Mail Acceptance Clerk. The Postal Service will provide a cardboard mail tray for your use.

Mail one to yourself, to make sure they're being delivered and when, and when you get it, study it for any improvements that can be made before the next printing, when you start out with another blank page.

SUMMARY

1. Mailers can be addressed by hand or photo copied labels.

2. To locate help, check the Yellow Pages under "Mailing Services" and "Secretarial Services."

3. Request a copy of Publication 113 from the U.S. Postal Service. Study it before sending out and/or designing your mailer.

4. To compute the approximate savings, if any, between First Class and bulk rate use this formula:

	FIRST CLASS	BULK
No. of pieces:	————	————
Postage each piece:	X————	X ————
No. mailings/year:	X————	X ————
Bulk permit fee:	+____.00	+ ————
TOTAL POSTAGE:	$————	$ ————

Typical bulk mail permit imprints. Make your own by using transfer lettering.

BULK RATE
U.S. Postage
PAID
Seattle, WA.
Permit No.

Nonprofit
Organization
U.S. Postage
PAID
American Lung
Association

Write to AVERY for more information on address labels

Address Labels for Copiers
eliminates repeat typing of mailing lists.

Copier Labels eliminate repeat typing of mailing lists.

Appendix

GRAPHIC ARTS SUPPLIES

Dick Blick   (Catalog $2.00)
Route 150 East
Galesburg, Illinois 61401

Creative Media Services
P. O. Box 5955-PP
Berkeley, California 94705

Dot Pasteup Supply
P. O. Box 369
Omaha, Nebraska 68101

Dynamic Graphics, Inc.
6000 North Forest Park Drive
Peoria, Illinois 61614-3592

Fidelity Graphic Arts Catalog
P. O. Box 155
Minneapolis, Minnesota 55440

Graphic Products Corporation
(Formatt, etc).
3601 Edison Place
Rolling Meadows, Illinois 60008-1062

Letraset USA
40 Eisenhower Drive
Paramus, New Jersey 07653

P O Instrument Co., Inc.
(Proedge)
Maple Grange Road
Box 888
Vernon, New Jersey 07462

The Printers Shopper   (free catalog)
P. O. Drawer 1056
Chula Vista, California 92012

Zipatone
150 Fencl Lane
Hillside, Illinois 60162

BUSINESS FORMS & SUPPLIES

The Business Book
Miles Kimball Company
One East Eighth Avenue
Oshkosh, Wisconsin 54901

Colwell Systems, Inc.
201 Kenyon Road
Champaign, Illinois 61820

The Drawing Board
256 Regal Row
P. O. Box 660429
Dallas, Texas 75266-0429

Fidelity Products Company
5601 International Parkway
P. O. Box 155
Minneapolis, Minnesota 55440

NEBS
New England Business Service
500 Main Street
Groton, Massachusetts 01471

The Stationery House, Inc.
1000 Florida Avenue
Hagerstown, Maryland 21741

MAILING LISTS

Dunhill International List Co., Inc.
1100 Park Central Blvd. South
Pompano Beach, Florida 33064-2213

Zeller & Letica, Inc.
15 East 26th Street
New York, New York 10010

MISCELLANEOUS

Avery International Company
777 East Foothill Blvd.
Azusa, California 91702

Eastman Kodak Company
175 Humbolt Street
Rochester, New York 14610-1099

Konica Business Machines U.S.A., Inc.
500 Day Hill Road
Windsor, Connecticut 06095

Polycor Corporation
1258 - 1st Avenue South
Seattle, Washington 98134

U.S. Small Business Administration
P. O. Box 15434
Fort Worth, Texas   76116

The names and addresses herein are listed
as a courtesy and convenience. The reader
is expected to employ consumer awareness
when dealing with any mail order firm.

SUGGESTED READING

HOW TO ADVERTISE AND PROMOTE YOUR RETAIL STORE
by Dana K. Cassell, American Management
Associations, New York

HOW TO MANAGE A RETAIL STORE
by J. Wingate & S. Helfant, Coles Publishing Company, Toronto, Canada

HOW TO START YOUR OWN CRAFT BUSINESS
by Herb Genfan & Lyn Taetzsch, Watson-
Guptill Publications, New York

PROMOTING & SELLING YOUR ART
by Carole Katchen, Watson-Guptill Publications, New York

PUBLISHING NEWSLETTERS
by Howard Penn Hudson, Charles Scribner's
Sons, New York

Hints and Tips

The following hints and tips on handling self-adhesive materials is provided by Letraset USA

CREATIVE TECHNIQUES

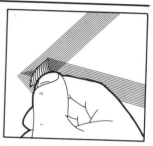

Since Letratone® patterns are printed on the surface, they can be scraped with a blade or manipulated with solvent to produce highlights. An extravagant range of Moire patterns can also be produced by simply overlaying films of varying tints and patterns.

Where two pieces of film must butt tightly, the films should be cut oversize and overlapped in position. Press lightly to fix in position, then cut through the two layers of film with a sharp knife.

Peel back both films from the immediate area of the cut and remove the excess film. Smooth down the cut films and the edges will meet. Burnish firmly for a strong bond.

SUITABLE SURFACES

Self-adhesive films and papers may be applied to most smooth and moderately smooth surfaces. Waxy or oily surfaces found in certain linens and papers (including certain types of diazo papers) repel many adhesives and may prevent the formation of a strong bond.

Extremely coarse or open grained boards and papers should also be avoided. They give poor adhesion, contribute to unsightly air bubbles and cause problems in photographic reproduction.

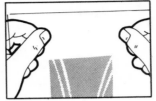

Atlernatively, coarse rulings can produce similar effects when placed on the underside of the drafting film. When dot for dot or discrete reproduction of screen tints is needed it is advisable to use tints with coarse rulings, e.g. 30 lines/inch.

PHOTOGRAPHIC

All the films and papers can be used in continuous tone photography and line reproduction. Color sheets photograph cleanly—the matt surface giving better reproduction than the glossy. They are also excellent for original art intended as reflective copy. For best reproduction of Letratone sheets, it is recommended that the artwork be produced oversize and shot with reflected light.

DIAZO

All the adhesives are heat-resistant and specifically designed to withstand diazo and dyeline copying. For Letratone sheets, shading and continuous tone effects are best achieved with the finer line rulings, e.g. 85 lines to the inch.

LARGE AREA APPLICATION

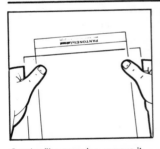

Cut the film over-size, remove it from the backing sheet and place it on top of a Letraset blue backing sheet. Slide the film over the top edge of the backing sheet and tack it into position.

Apply the rest of the film by slowly moving the backing sheet down the artwork while at the same time smoothing the film by hand or with a soft cloth. Once the film is in position, burnish it firmly.

The following tips are provided
by Graphics Products Corporation

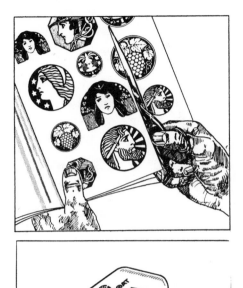

1. Select an attention-
getting illustration
or graphic element

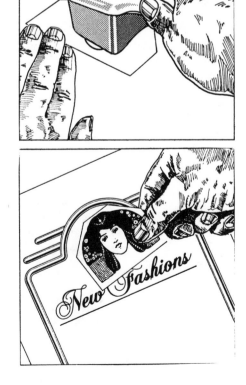

2. Apply adhesive to
the back of the art
and trim away excess
paper

3. Position element
into place on artwork,
cover with protective
overlay, and burnish
into place

ADD YOUR OWN IDEAS QUICKLY AND EASILY

Ink in backgrounds or areas of the
illustrations for increased visual impact

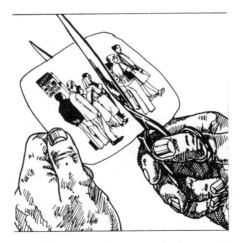

Crop and edit to fit special needs
or space requirements

Add FORMATT shading film to enhance
or highlight areas

TIME SAVING APPLICATION OF FORMATT RULES

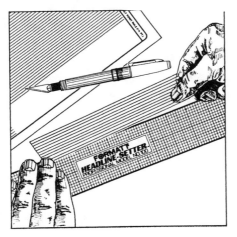

1. Cut out a section of rules from a
FORMATT sheet and attach bottom line
along the edge of a HEADLINE SETTER

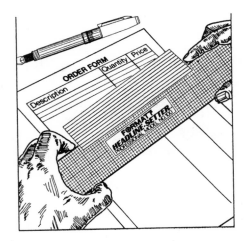

2. Position rule along leading edge of section on artwork and smooth into place with finger

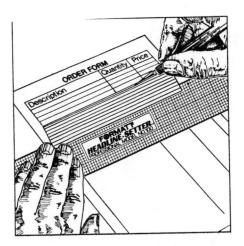

3. Trim away section of rules remaining on the HEADLINE SETTER and then thoroughly burnish rule positioned on artwork

1. Produce clean, mitered corners by overlapping the ends of each border at all corners.

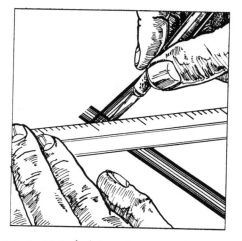

2. Lay a straight edge on the over-lapped area and cut carefully through both film layers.

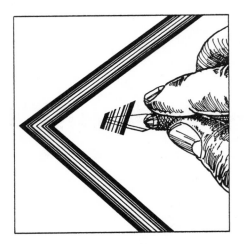

3. Carefully remove the excess border film and firmly burnish the mitered corners into place

ADHESIVE WAX APPLICATOR

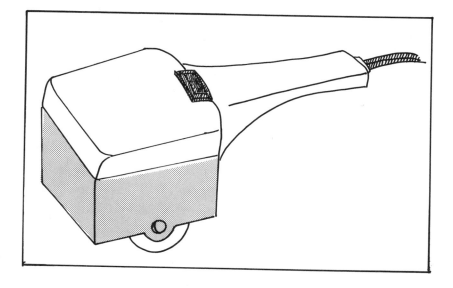

The illustration above shows a typical hand held adhesive wax applicator, a basic tool of many graphic and commercial artists.

Wax applicators are used to put a micro thin layer of adhesive wax on the back of copy and artwork for pasteup. To use a wax applicator, simply insert a few small bars of specially formulated wax, plug in the electrical cord, and allow the wax to melt. When the wax is melted, roll the applicator over the back of the copy or artwork, trim away excess margins, and position on your pasteup board.

Waxed copy and artwork can be lifted and repositioned numerous times before final burnishing and often even afterward!

The applicators are priced from $45 and up, and offer the following benefits:

+ fast coating and pasteup

+ easy positioning of paper

+ easy refilling

+ easy to peel off and reapply

+ environmentally safe

+ odorless

+ quick drying

+ stainproof on ordinary pasteup
  materials

+ cheaper than rubber cement

+ better hold than rubber cement

+ cleaner and neater than rubber
  cement

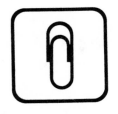

Index